The MAILBOX® — The Education Center®

Language Arts

W9-COW-482

Practice Galore

Skill-Based Puzzle Pages

- Phonics
- Word Skills
- Vocabulary
- Parts of Speech
- Punctuation
- Capitalization

Written by Laura Mihalenko

Managing Editor: Hope Taylor Spencer

Editorial Team: Becky S. Andrews, Kimberley Bruck, Sharon Murphy, Debra Liverman, Diane Badden, Thad H. McLaurin, Jennifer Bragg, Sherry McGregor, Karen A. Brudnak, Jennifer Nunn, Hope Rodgers, Dorothy C. McKinney

Production Team: Lori Z. Henry, Pam Crane, Rebecca Saunders, Chris Curry, Sarah Foreman, Theresa Lewis Goode, Greg D. Rieves, Eliseo De Jesus Santos II, Barry Slate, Donna K. Teal, Zane Williard, Kitty Campbell, Tazmen Carlisle, Kathy Coop, Marsha Heim, Lynette Dickerson, Mark Rainey, Karen Brewer Grossman

Fun, independent skill practice!

www.themailbox.com

Manufactured in the United States
10 9 8 7 6 5 4 3 2 1

Table of Contents

Phonics

Language Conventions

Word Skills and Vocabulary

Arctic Acrobat

Write *a* or *e* to complete each word.
Circle the words in the puzzle.

S	T	A	N	D	S	B	G	D
T	E	D	A	S	H	E	S	A
R	K	E	B	F	K	T	C	N
E	X	P	E	R	T	D	A	T
T	H	E	N	F	B	S	T	A
C	H	F	S	P	J	N	C	R
H	A	L	E	G	S	A	H	C
I	C	A	C	R	O	B	A	T
N	T	P	O	S	M	U	Q	I
G	O	S	N	C	R	T	C	C
B	E	N	D	S	G	M	L	A
I	P	L	A	N	N	I	N	G
B	E	S	T	K	E	P	T	Y

1. Pablo Penguin is an __xpert __crobat.

2. First, he warms up by str__tching his l__gs.

3. S__cond, he fl__ps his fins.

4. Th__n he d__shes about doing his tricks.

5. He b__nds and flips, and then st__nds on his head.

6. Pablo is the South Pole's b__st-k__pt secret.

7. Are you pl__nning a trip to __ntarctica?

8. Be sure to c__tch his __ct!

NAME _____

• A Sweet Birthday •

How old is Princess?

Write *i* or *o* to complete each word.
Color each short *i* word red.
Color each short *o* word yellow.

b__x	l__d	m__p	f__sh	r__ch	g__ft	h__nk
bl__ck	m__lk	pl__p	fr__g	p__nd	d__p	l__ng
r__cket	w__ng	fl__ss	th__s	sw__ng	tr__ck	m__m
m__th	br__ng	up__n	h__m	h__pping	d__t	s__cks
st__p	tr__p	s__ccer	h__d	ch__n	w__sh	fr__st

• Short vowels i, o • 5

On the Way

Circle each word with the short *u* sound.
Then trace the path to help Sid get to the circus.

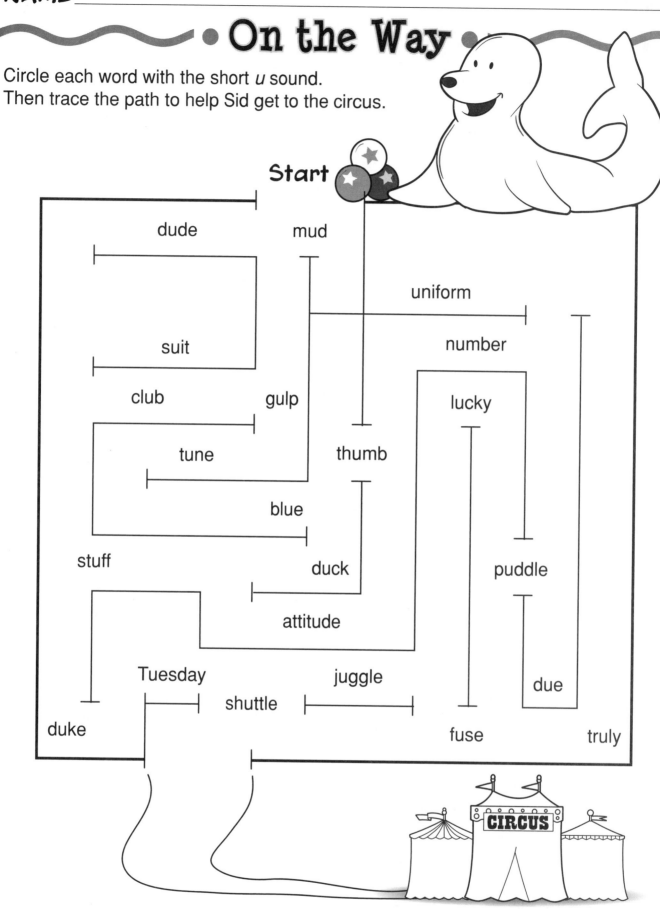

Start

dude   mud

uniform

number

suit

club   gulp

lucky

tune   thumb

blue

stuff   duck   puddle

attitude

Tuesday   juggle

shuttle   due

duke   fuse   truly

CIRCUS

Let the Good Times Roll

Write a long *a* word for each "Across" clue.
Write a long *e* word for each "Down" clue.

Across
1. a dish
3. opposite of give
5. not on time
7. a hammer hits this
9. let out the water
11. not nights

Down
2. opposite of west
4. snakelike fish
6. not odd
8. opposite of follow
10. must have
12. look

• Take to the Skies •

Write *i, o,* or *u* to complete each word.
Color by the code.

Color Code
long *i* = blue
long *o* = yellow
long *u* = green

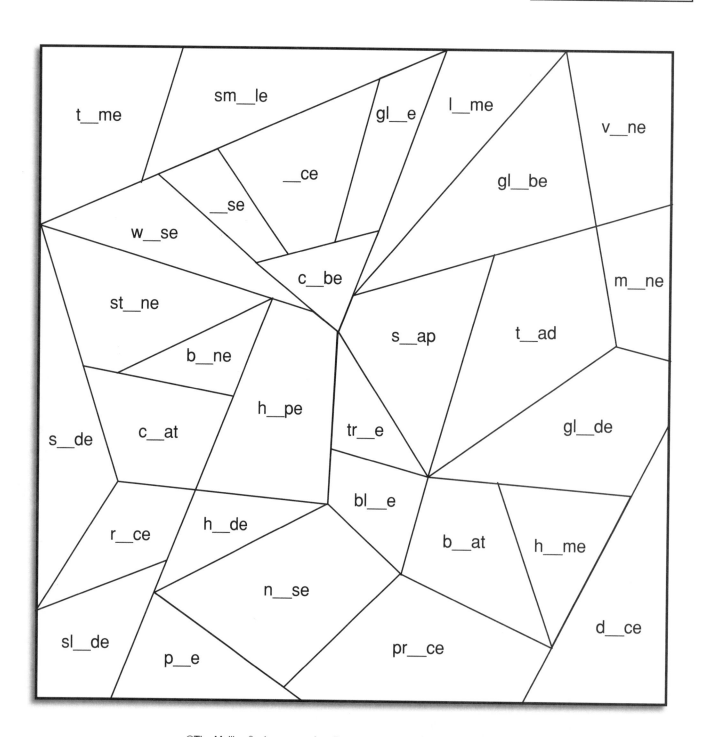

sm__le
t__me
gl__e
l__me
v__ne
__ce
gl__be
__se
w__se
c__be
m__ne
st__ne
s__ap
t__ad
b__ne
h__pe
s__de
c__at
tr__e
gl__de
bl__e
h__de
r__ce
b__at
h__me
n__se
d__ce
sl__de
p__e
pr__ce

Some Rest and Relaxation

Write the short *a* word that matches the first clue.
Then make one change to the word to make a word that matches the next clue.
Repeat for each clue.

1. this and _____ ☐☐a☐

2. something that keeps the head warm ☐☐a☐

3. an animal that meows ☐☐a☐

4. a small rug ☐☐a☐

5. a grown-up boy ☐a☐

6. a tool that moves air to cool you ☐a☐

7. a tool for cooking ☐a☐

8. a light-brown color ☐a☐

9. to touch lightly ☐a☐

10. a drawing that shows places ☐a☐

11. to sleep for just a bit ☐a☐

12. a cracking sound ☐☐a☐

• **Word families *an, ap, at*** • 9

Frolicking Friends

Write *ide*, *ight*, or *ine* to complete each word.
Write the new words in the puzzle.

Across

2. Last n_____, Sara and Sammi played games.
4. The moon and stars were br_____.
6. They played h_____-and-seek.
8. Sammi hid in a p_____ tree.
10. Sara hid behind a w_____ log.

Down

1. Sammi and Sara found a hanging v_____.
3. They both held on t_____.
5. Then they let it gl_____ through the air.
7. What a r_____!
9. "I'm glad you're my friend," said Sammi.
   "And I'm glad you're m_____," answered Sara.

A "Ruff" Day's Work

Write *eat*, *ell*, or *est* to complete each word.
Circle each word in the puzzle.

r	l	e	m	o	y	t	g	r
s	l	i	n	e	h	r	e	e
l	e	m	u	l	e	l	h	s
m	s	e	c	l	p	t	z	t
p	t	c	j	l	q	o	r	e
e	a	t	a	e	h	w	d	w
s	y	b	k	g	i	n	a	e
t	v	t	s	e	n	t	c	x

1. r _ _ _ _

2. sp _ _ _ _

3. v _ _ _ _

4. y _ _ _ _ ow

5. _ _ _ _ ing

6. tr _ _ _ _

7. sm _ _ _ _

8. m _ _ _ _

9. wh _ _ _ _

10. sh _ _ _ _

11. p _ _ _ _

12. cont _ _ _ _

Word families *eat, ell, est* • 11

Pizza Time!

What kind of pizza do kangaroos like best?

Write the word for each clue.

Hint: Each word will have *ock*, *op*, or *ot* in it.

1. the opposite of cold

2. a thin, straight opening

3. a place where things are sold

4. a large stone

5. a small stain

6. the opposite of go

7. to have shut with a key

8. to let something fall

9. clothing for a foot

10. _____ at all

Write each boxed letter from above in order below.

I ' ___ " ___ — ___ I " !

• Home, "Tweet" Home •

Help each bird find the path to its house.
In each column, add *sp*, *sc*, or *sw* to the letters that make a word.

	ale	__ in	__ ider	__ ace	__ arf	__ eed	__ eep
sc	scale						
sp							
sw							

	__ im	__ arm	__ ort	__ eak	__ ing	__ ark	__ alp
sc							
sp							
sw							

• Farming the Fields •

Write *br, pr,* or *tr* to complete a word.

1. John is a __ __ oduce farmer.

2. He loves to ride on his __ __ actor.

3. He __ __ ies to be outside by sunrise.

4. Then he __ __ avels through his fields.

5. His tractor turns the dark __ __ own soil.

6. John loves the __ __ ight sunshine.

7. He also likes the warm __ __ eezes.

8. He smiles as he __ __ epares the fields.

9. John takes __ __ ide in his work.

Which cornstalk will grow the fastest?

Color one section from the stalk for each matching blend.

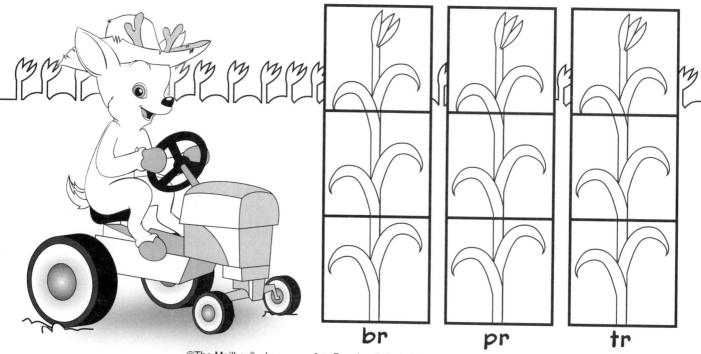

br   pr   tr

It Takes Teamwork

Write a word that ends with *nd* or *nt* and matches the first clue.
Then make one change to the word to make a word that ends with *nd* or *nt*
   and matches the next clue.
Repeat for each clue.

1. a very small, strong insect

2. also

3. Earth's soil

4. the opposite of borrow

5. to mail a letter

6. to have already mailed a letter

7. crooked

8. the opposite of came

9. to wish for

10. a magician's stick

11. used to build castles at the beach

12. the opposite of sit

• Time for Bed •

Write *ft*, *lp*, or *st* to complete each word.
Write the new words in the puzzle.

Across

2. Molly is going to re___ ___.
4. She wants to fall fa___ ___ asleep.
5. She mu___ ___ get ready first.
6. She drinks a gu___ ___ of water.
8. She brushes her cowhide until it is so___ ___.
10. She helps her sister put on her pajamas fir___ ___.

Down

1. Before she dri___ ___s off, she will read a book.
3. She will he___ ___ her sister read one too.
7. There is nothing le___ ___ to do but go to sleep.
9. Molly twi___ ___s her blanket and begins to dream!

NAME_____

How will the bear get to the honey?

Write *ch* or *th* to complete each word.

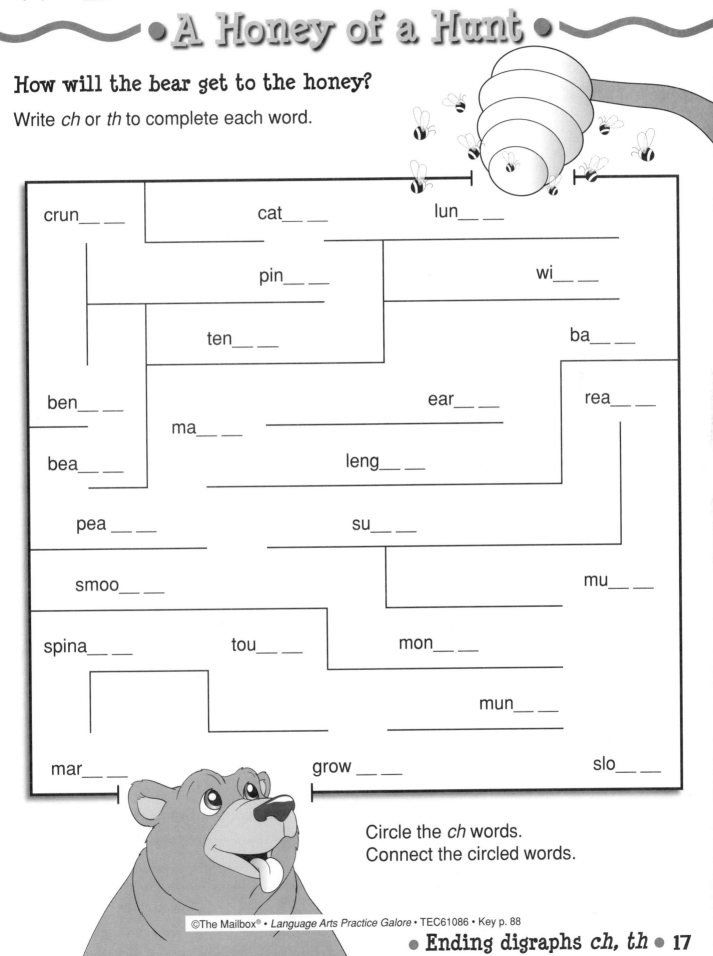

crun___ ___

cat___ ___

lun___ ___

pin___ ___

wi___ ___

ten___ ___

ba___ ___

ben___ ___

ma___ ___

ear___ ___

rea___ ___

bea___ ___

leng___ ___

pea ___ ___

su___ ___

smoo___ ___

mu___ ___

spina___ ___

tou___ ___

mon___ ___

mun___ ___

mar___ ___

grow ___ ___

slo___ ___

Circle the *ch* words.
Connect the circled words.

• Scattered Shoes •

Show the path Lucy takes to gather her missing shoes.

Write *sh* or *th* to complete each word.
Color by the code.

Color Code
words that end with *sh* = green
words that end with *th* = yellow

mon___	tra___	pu___	flu___	a___	spla___
clo___	fi___	tee___	fif___	tru___	wrea___
four___	bo___	mou___	bru___	fla___	ten___
bu___	ca___	slu___	di___	wa___	six___
ear___	nin___	blu___	da___	la___	too___
ra___	nor___	pa___	heal___	boo___	sou___

©The Mailbox® • *Language Arts Practice Galore* • TEC61086 • Key p. 88

18 • **Ending digraphs *sh, th*** •

Riding the Waves

Write a word that contains *ir* or *ar* on the snail's shell.
Use the clues to help you.
The last letter of each word will be the first letter of the next.

1. a place where clowns perform
2. a long strip of cloth worn around the neck
3. a place where animals live and crops are grown
4. to walk with regular steps, as in a parade
5. difficult
6. soil
7. after second
8. a small arrow
9. how you feel when you want a drink
10. thick string used to knit

1. Ⓒ i r c u Ⓢ

• *R*-controlled vowels *ar, ir* • 19

©The Mailbox® • *Language Arts Practice Galore* • TEC61086 • Key p. 88

• Changes on the Farm •

Write *or* or *ur* to complete each word.
Circle each new word in the puzzle.

1. Farmer Brown was w__ __ried about his pony, Popcorn.

2. Last Th__ __sday, he noticed something odd.

3. The pony's mane and tail were p__ __ple!

4. There was another change the next m__ __ning.

5. Popcorn's coat had t__ __ned from brown to white.

6. Well, he knew that wasn't n__ __mal!

7. Farmer Brown h__ __ried to call the vet.

8. By the time the vet arrived, there was one m__ __e change.

9. What a s__ __prise!

10. Popcorn had grown a h__ __n.

11. "I don't know what you were feeding your h__ __se," said the vet.

12. "But now you've got a unic__ __ n!"

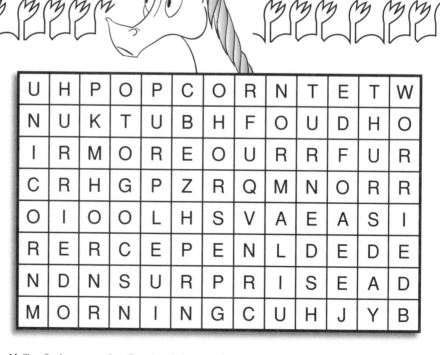

U	H	P	O	P	C	O	R	N	T	E	T	W
N	U	K	T	U	B	H	F	O	U	D	H	O
I	R	M	O	R	E	O	U	R	R	F	U	R
C	R	H	G	P	Z	R	Q	M	N	O	R	R
O	I	O	O	L	H	S	V	A	E	A	S	I
R	E	R	C	E	P	E	N	L	D	E	D	E
N	D	N	S	U	R	P	R	I	S	E	A	D
M	O	R	N	I	N	G	C	U	H	J	Y	B

Mysteries of the Deep

Use the code to write each missing word.

1. Have you heard of people who live _____?

2. When I walk on the beach, I _____.

3. Could a _____ be hiding there?

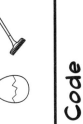

4. I will find out this _____.

5. I will _____ the truth.

6. I will be an _____, underwater detective!

Code

a	c	d	e	i	m	n	o	r	s	t	u	v	w

• What a Pearl! •

Write *oi* or *oy* to complete each word.
Circle the *oi* words.
Connect the circled words to get to the center of the pearl.

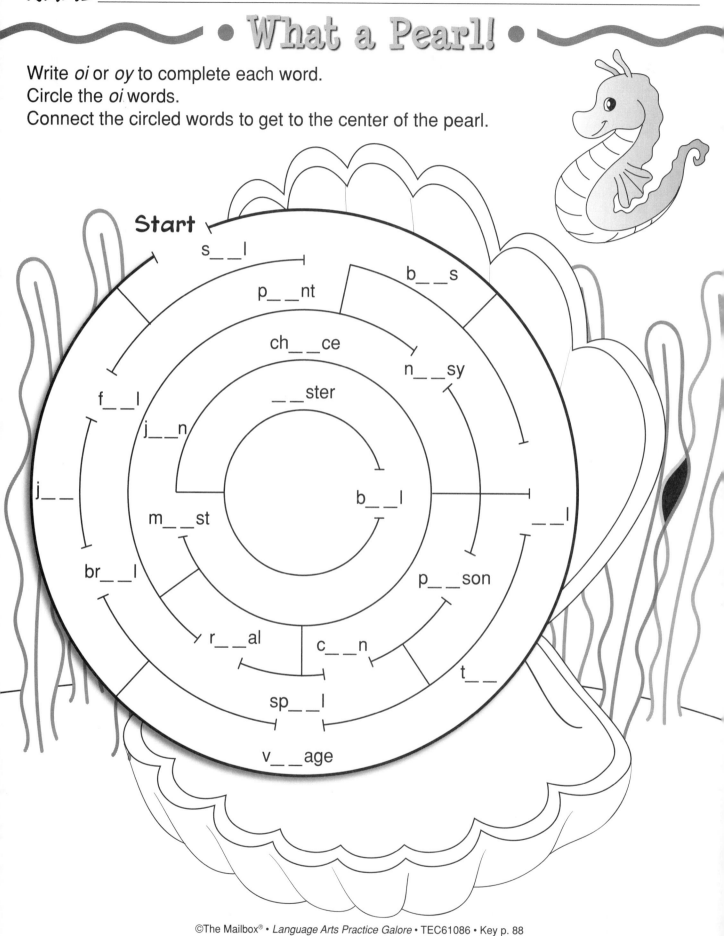

Start

s _ _ l

p _ _ nt

b _ _ s

ch _ _ ce

n _ _ sy

_ _ ster

f _ _ l

j _ _ n

j _ _

b _ _ l

_ _ l

m _ _ st

br _ _ l

p _ _ son

r _ _ al

c _ _ n

t _ _

sp _ _ l

v _ _ age

Blowing Bubbles

Circle the correct word in each pair.
For each *ou* word, color one of Willy's bubbles.
For each *ow* word, color one of Wanda's bubbles.

1. about	abowt	7. pouer	power
2. house	howse	8. south	sowth
3. toun	town	9. shouer	shower
4. round	rownd	10. groul	growl
5. found	fownd	11. proud	prowd
6. froun	frown	12. allou	allow

WANDA

ow

WILLY

ou

©The Mailbox® • *Language Arts Practice Galore* • TEC61086 • Key p. 88

• Monkey Business •

What does Matilda say about life as a yo-yo champ?

Decide which part of each sentence is underlined.
Circle the letter in the matching column.

	Subject	Predicate	Neither
1. Matilda is a monkey.	K	S	D
2. She lives in the jungle.	I	L	R
3. Matilda likes swinging in the trees.	N	E	D
4. Yellow bananas are her favorite food.	O	A	G
5. Many monkeys swing and eat bananas.	B	S	W
6. But Matilda is special.	M	T	F
7. She knows how to yo-yo!	H	N	O
8. Matilda can hold a yo-yo in each hand.	U	T	E
9. Her tail can hold a third yo-yo!	R	C	P
10. Matilda's tricks are amazing!	A	J	Q

Now write the circled letters above on the numbered lines below.

___ ___ has ___ ___ ___   ___ ___ ___   ___ ___ ___   ___ ___ ___ ___ ___!
 2   6   2   6   1   8   9   1   10   7   3   3   4   5   7   1

NAME_____

Splish, Splash!

Which bird likes to take a bath more than any other?

Color the triangle that is between each sentence's subject and predicate.

1. The neighborhood \C/ birds \A/ are all aflutter.

2. A new \K/ surprise \P/ is here.

3. Mrs. Briar \T/ put a birdbath \D/ in her garden.

4. It \B/ is \U/ beautiful!

5. The birds \L/ are \R/ all lining up.

6. The chickadees \O/ have brought \B/ their own towels.

7. A cardinal \M/ brought \R/ some bubble bath.

8. Feathers \T/ are flying with \E/ excitement.

9. Tweeting \I/ can be \B/ heard all over.

10. The birds \R/ hope Mrs. Briar will remember to put \U/ water in the birdbath.

Now write the uncolored letters above on the numbered lines below.

A ___ ___ ___ ___ ___ ___   ___ ___ ___ ___
   7   10   9   6   8   5   3   4   1   2

• Roaring Racecars •

Which car will cross the finish line first?

Color the circled letter under each word that is capitalized correctly.
Color a section of racetrack in front of the car with the matching letter.

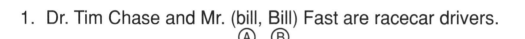

1. Dr. Tim Chase and Mr. (bill, Bill) Fast are racecar drivers.
   Ⓐ Ⓑ

2. (Dr., dr.) Chase's car is bright blue.
   Ⓐ Ⓑ

3. Mr. (Fast, fast) drives a red car.
   Ⓐ   Ⓑ

4. Dr. Chase's son, (mark, Mark), helps his dad.
   Ⓐ   Ⓑ

5. The racetrack mechanic is (Mrs., mrs.) Swift.
   Ⓐ   Ⓑ

6. Mrs. Swift helps (Bill, bill) and Tim keep their cars running.
   Ⓐ Ⓑ

7. The man who pumps the gasoline is (mr., Mr.) Quick.
   Ⓐ Ⓑ

8. Mr. Quick has a helper named (Tammy, tammy).
   Ⓐ   Ⓑ

9. Mr. (quick, Quick) and Tammy work hard at the track.
   Ⓐ   Ⓑ

10. Dr. Chase and (mr., Mr.) Fast have lots of help, and they're ready to race!
    Ⓐ Ⓑ

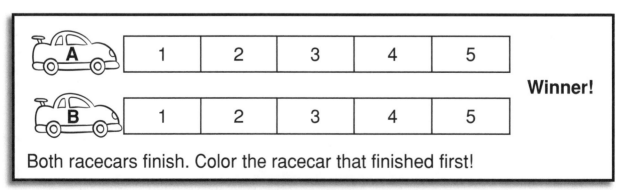

A	1	2	3	4	5
B	1	2	3	4	5

Winner!

Both racecars finish. Color the racecar that finished first!

• The Most Special Day •

Color the puzzle pieces that are capitalized correctly.
Cut out the colored pieces.
Glue.

Hint: Glue the pieces in order on the cake.

wednesday	friday
Tuesday	Monday
thursday	Saturday
Friday	tuesday
monday	Thursday
Sunday	sunday
saturday	Wednesday

• Capitalization: days of the week • 27

NAME _____

• Month by Month •

What's the difference between January 1 and December 31?

Color each letter that has a word on it that is capitalized incorrectly.

©The Mailbox® • Language Arts Practice Galore • TEC61086 • Key p. 89

NAME_____

• 'Tis the Season! •

Cut apart the squares at the bottom of the page.
Find the squares with holiday names that are capitalized correctly.
Glue each one on its matching picture.

	Valentine's Day	fourth Of July		St. Patrick's Day
St. patrick's Day			halloween	
	hanukkah	Fourth of July		columbus day
Columbus Day			thanksgiving	
				easter
Easter	Kwanzaa	Valentine's day	Halloween	
Thanksgiving		Hanukkah		kwanzaa
	New year's Eve		New Year's Eve	

NAME_____

• To the Top! •

How will the climber reach the top?

Circle each place name that is correctly capitalized or does not need to be capitalized. Connect the circled words.

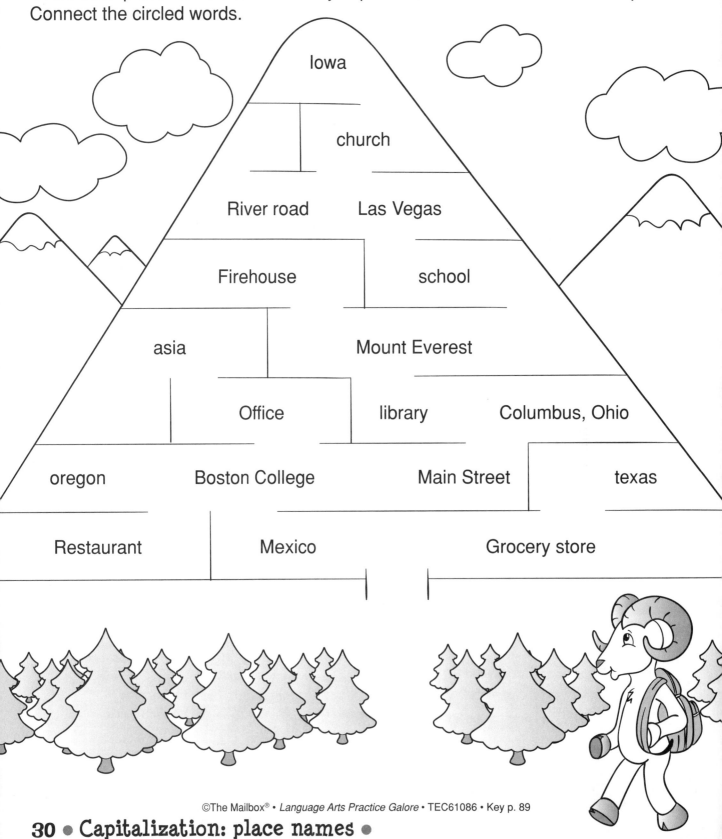

Iowa

church

River road   Las Vegas

Firehouse   school

asia   Mount Everest

Office   library   Columbus, Ohio

oregon   Boston College   Main Street   texas

Restaurant   Mexico   Grocery store

©The Mailbox® • Language Arts Practice Galore • TEC61086 • Key p. 89

A Mouthful of Mail

Circle each letter that should be capitalized but is not.
Write the number of circled letters on each stamp.
Add the numbers across and down. Each sum should be the same number.

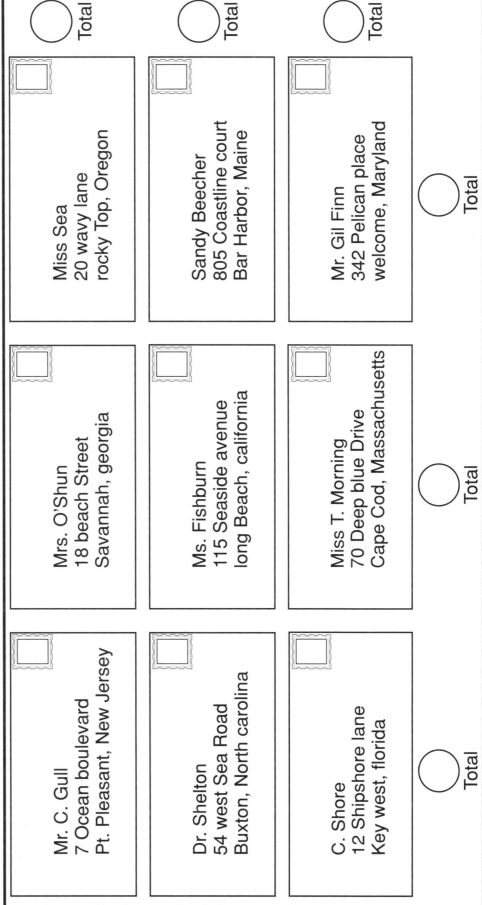

Mr. C. Gull
7 Ocean boulevard
Pt. Pleasant, New Jersey

Mrs. O'Shun
18 beach Street
Savannah, georgia

Miss Sea
20 wavy lane
rocky Top, Oregon

Total

Dr. Shelton
54 west Sea Road
Buxton, North carolina

Ms. Fishburn
115 Seaside avenue
long Beach, california

Sandy Beecher
805 Coastline court
Bar Harbor, Maine

Total

C. Shore
12 Shipshore lane
Key west, florida

Miss T. Morning
70 Deep blue Drive
Cape Cod, Massachusetts

Mr. Gil Finn
342 Pelican place
welcome, Maryland

Total

Total   Total   Total

Beautiful Dreamers

Where do roses sleep?

Write each ending punctuation mark.
Color the punctuation mark on its matching puzzle square.
Use the code to help you solve the riddle.

1. Wow, your roses are beautiful ___

2. What color are they ___

3. They are red and yellow ___

4. I want to plant a pink rose too ___

5. What do you do to take care of them ___

6. I give them water and plant food ___

7. Wow, I really like to look at them ___

8. May I smell the red one ___

9. Look out, there's a bee on that one ___

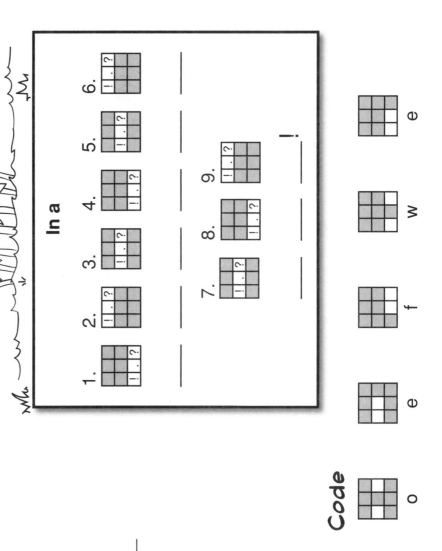

In a

1.   2.   3.   4.   5.   6.

7.   8.   9.

_____ !

Code

d	r	l	b	o	e	f	w	e

A World Traveler

Color the correct end mark.
Make a path from Harry to his hotel.

	!	.	?
1. Boy, Harry loves to travel	!	.	?
2. He has been all over Africa and Asia	!	.	?
3. Have you ever been to a different country	!	.	?
4. You need to get a passport before you go	!	.	?
5. Your passport is stamped in each country you visit	!	.	?
6. Wow, Harry's passport has 43 stamps	!	.	?
7. He'll need a new one soon	!	.	?
8. Do you travel like Harry does	!	.	?
9. Harry travels by plane, train, and boat	!	.	?
10. All of this traveling makes him tired	!	.	?
11. Can you guess where Harry will go next	!	.	?
12. I think he'll go to sleep	!	.	?

Hippo Hotel

• Fast Food •

What's in Charlie's bag?

To find out, cut out the boxes below the sentences on the left.
Glue each box beside the type of sentence it names.
Then repeat for the sentences on the right.

Would you rather eat at home?		
Call Charlie and place an order.		
Charlie delivers all of the food himself.		
Wow, that is *fast* food!		

Charlie just opened a restaurant.		
Have you seen the menu?		
There are so many choices!		
Try today's special.		

statement	command	exclamation	question

question	exclamation	command	statement

Say Cheese!

For each sentence, write *statement, question, command,* or *exclamation* in the puzzle.

Across
2. Cheese is my favorite food.
5. Take a picture of me with the cheese.
7. I can hardly wait to eat some.
8. Have you ever seen so much cheese?
9. Don't start eating yet.

Down
1. Did you take the picture?
3. I can hardly wait to dig in!
4. I think I heard a noise!
5. Hide!
6. Can we eat yet?

NAME_____

• Just Hopping Through •

How will the bunny get to the carrots?

Color each noun.

under	rabbit	book	farmer
garden	teacher	furry	dirt
quickly	many	joking	hop	school
animal	baby	home	ruler	child
car	lightly	handy	hot	eat
mother	wow	church	mailman	vegetable
pencil	folder	uncle	deeply	beach
grow	to	slowly	the	hat
crunchy	baker	carrot	playground	clown
small	seeds	is	in	sit

©The Mailbox® • *Language Arts Practice Galore* • TEC61086 • Key p. 90

NAME _____

• Sea Breeze •

Color by the code.

May

Truman School

Houston

Mr. Reed

September

water

sea

Labor Day

Jordan

people

leaf

planet

ship

Fran

Tuesday

bike

wrote

asked

windy

beautiful

took

always

when

summer

sand

Kevin

Florida

books

story

America

until

Main Street

Amy

to

July

Pacific Ocean

Ms. Sanders

weather

©The Mailbox® • *Language Arts Practice Galore* • TEC61086 • Key p. 90

• Nouns • 37

Collecting Seashells

Color the puzzle pieces that have verbs on them.
Cut out the colored pieces.
Glue.

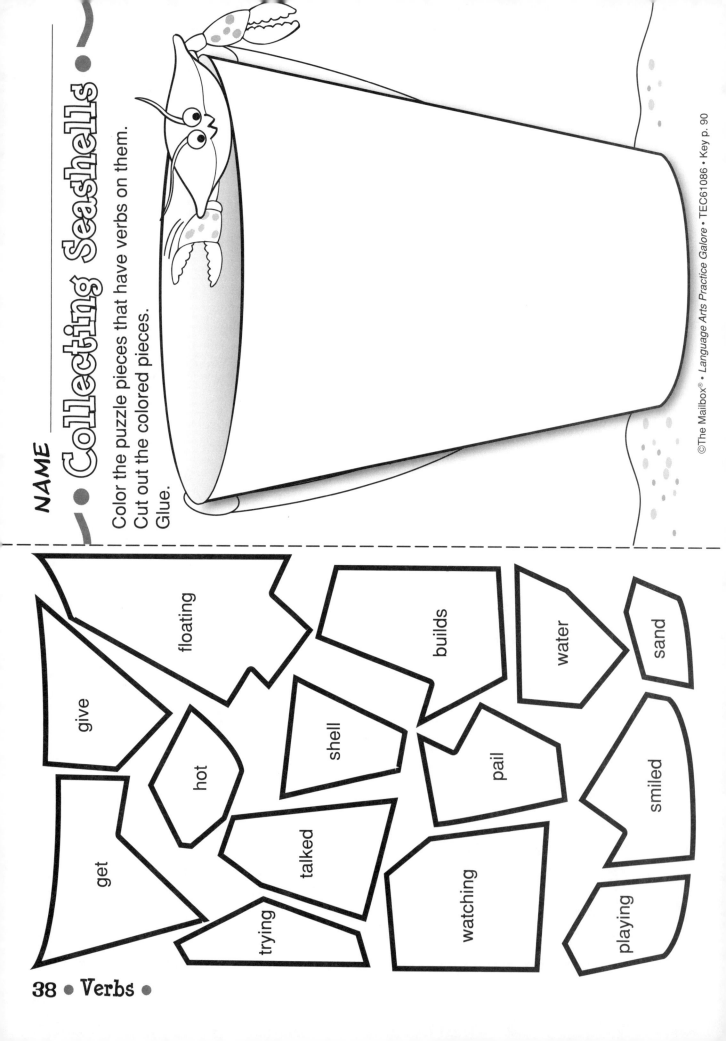

floating

give

hot

get

talked

trying

shell

watching

builds

pail

water

smiled

sand

playing

NAME_____

•A Speedy Getaway!•

How will the fly escape?

Circle each verb.
Connect the circled words.

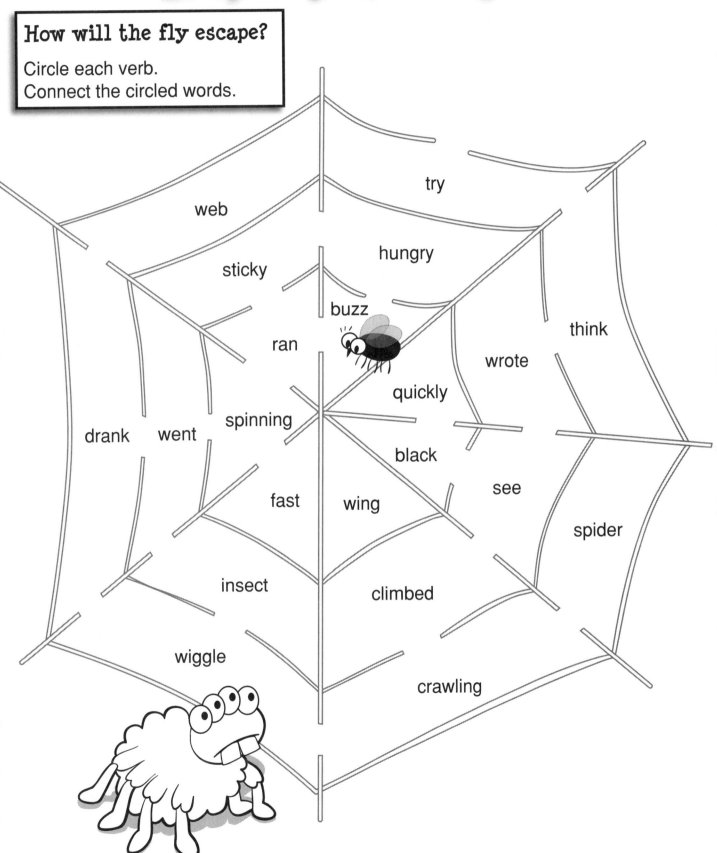

web

try

sticky

hungry

buzz

ran

think

wrote

quickly

drank   went   spinning

black

see

fast   wing

spider

insect   climbed

wiggle

crawling

NAME _____

• A Good Sport •

Decide which pronoun can take the place of each noun below.
Color by the code.

Color Code
she = green
he = brown
it = yellow
they = blue

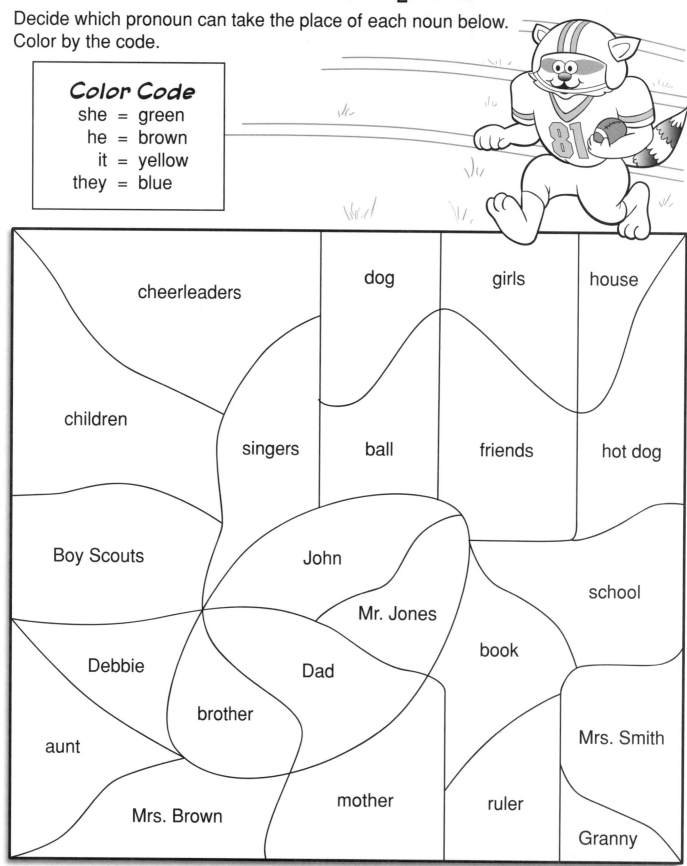

cheerleaders

dog

girls

house

children

singers

ball

friends

hot dog

Boy Scouts

John

Mr. Jones

school

Debbie

Dad

book

brother

Mrs. Smith

aunt

Mrs. Brown

mother

ruler

Granny

©The Mailbox® • *Language Arts Practice Galore* • TEC61086 • Key p. 90

Ring Around the Turtle

Circle each adjective.
Then write each adjective around the turtle's shell.
The last letter of one word will be the first letter of the next.

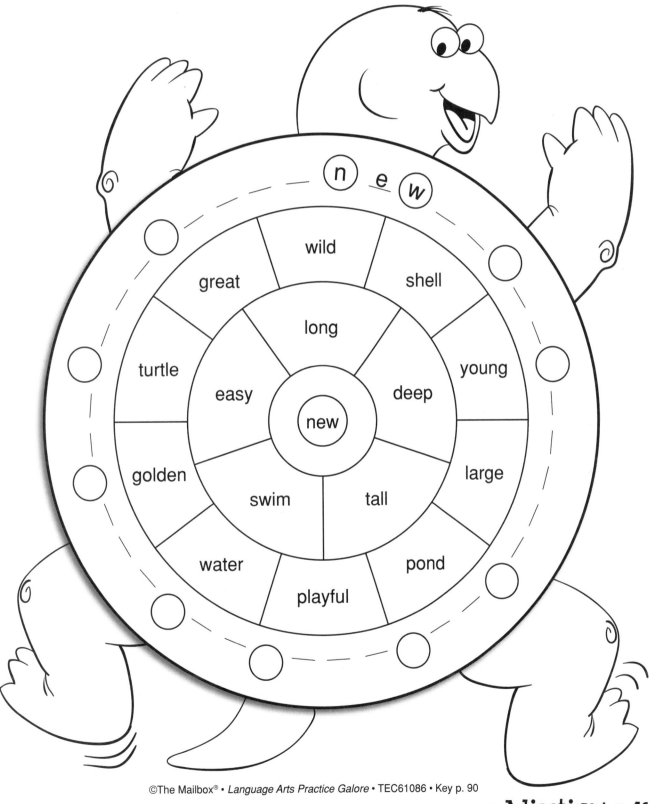

Searching the Sea

Where is the submarine going?

Color each box that has an adjective.

easy	waves	lonely	float	deep	tricky	four
several	bubbled	blue	freeze	little	hid	quiet
windy	keep	pleasant	do	some	salty	hot
cool	took	clever	him	pretty	sat	flipper
green	many	wet	sink	funny	breathe	see

Calendar Confusion

When should the sea horse go to dinner?

Circle each date that is punctuated correctly.
Connect the circled dates.

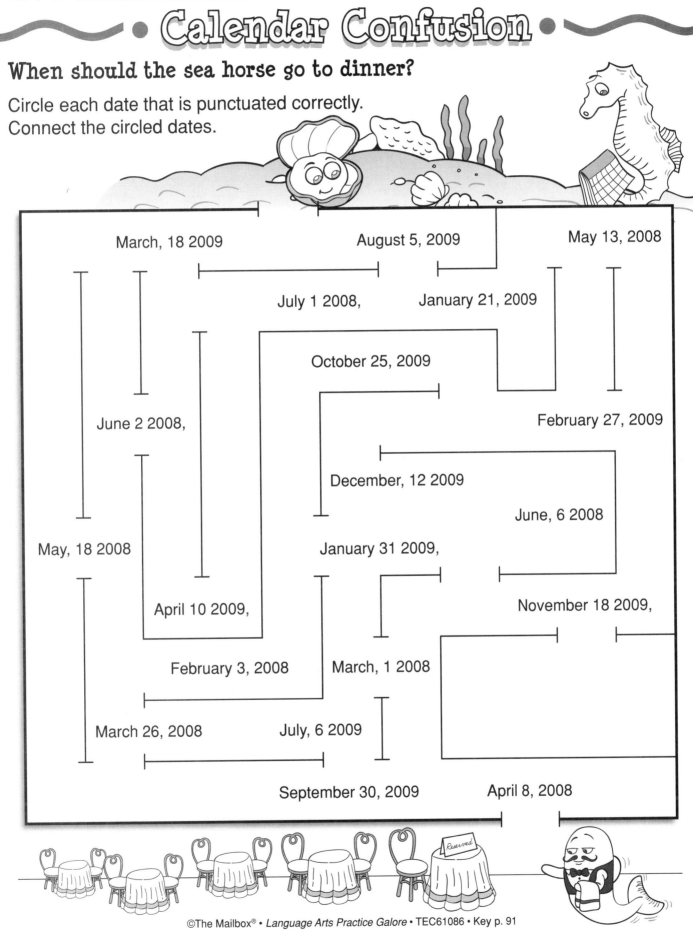

March, 18 2009

August 5, 2009

May 13, 2008

July 1 2008,

January 21, 2009

October 25, 2009

February 27, 2009

June 2 2008,

December, 12 2009

June, 6 2008

May, 18 2008

January 31 2009,

November 18 2009,

April 10 2009,

February 3, 2008

March, 1 2008

March 26, 2008

July, 6 2009

September 30, 2009

April 8, 2008

Cross-Country Camper

Rewrite each city and state from the tent on a matching line.
Use a comma to separate each city and state.

Sedona Arizona
Cottonwood California
Durango Colorado
Great Falls Montana
Valley of Fire Nevada
Santa Fe New Mexico
Salt Flat Texas

B r y c e   C a n y o n ,   U t a h

Now copy each word in a boldfaced box to find the
question Max was trying to answer at the campsites.

Can _____

©The Mailbox® • *Language Arts Practice Galore* • TEC61086 • Key p. 91

• Animal Asleep! •

What do you call a bull that can't stay awake?

To find out, read each sentence.
If the commas are correct, circle the letter in the "Yes" column.
If the commas are incorrect, circle the letter in the "No" column.

	Yes	No
1. Bob likes to spend his day resting, eating, and talking.	U	V
2. He likes, to rest in the barn, the field, and the farmhouse.	W	Z
3. He always has a blanket, pillow, and teddy bear with him.	A	G
4. *Warm, relaxed,* and *cozy* are his favorite words!	L	P
5. Bob likes to eat, grain, hay, and grass after a rest.	J	R
6. The, chickens, dogs and horses don't know how he can be so hungry.	K	B
7. They cluck, bark, and nay at him.	O	N
8. Bob just smiles, laughs, and talks, back to the animals.	T	L
9. He thinks life on the farm is fun, quiet, and relaxing.	E	H
10. You would too if you spent each day, resting eating, and talking!	F	D

Now write the circled letters above on the numbered lines below.

___ "___ ___ ___ ___ ___ ___ ___ ___ ___"
 3   6   1   8   4   10   7   2   9   5

• Undersea Circus •

Who are the funniest performers at the circus?

Underline each speaker's exact words.
Color the triangle to show where the missing quotation mark should go.

1. "Are you going to the circus? ▽E asked Shelly. ▽P

2. ▽F I would not ▽D miss it," said Sandy.

3. "The octopus is a great juggler! ▽C Shelly ▽G said.

4. Sandy said, ▽S Yes, ▽U he is amazing to see."

5. ▽R Shelly asked, "Which act is your favorite? ▽N

6. "That is hard to say, ▽T Sandy said. ▽J

7. ▽L I like when the shrimp ride ▽B the sea horses,"
   Shelly said.

8. "I like the lionfish tamer! ▽H Sandy said. ▽A

9. ▽W Well, ▽K what are we waiting for?" Shelly asked.

10. Sandy smiled ▽M and said, ▽I Let's go!"

Now write the colored letters above on the matching lines below.

___ ___ ___   ___ ___ O ___ ___ ___ ___ ___ ___
6   8   1   3   7   9   5   2 10   4   8

Tap-Dancing Tarantula

What is the only thing Tess doesn't like about tap dancing?

Underline each speaker's exact words.
If the quotation marks are correct, circle the letter in the "Yes" column.
If the quotation marks are incorrect, circle the letter in the "No" column.

	Yes	No
1. "How did you become a great dancer, Tess?" asked Tony.	E	C
2. Tess said, "Practice, practice, practice."	O	L
3. "But what made you choose tap?" Tony asked.	A	M
4. My mom helped me choose it "said Tess."	K	P
5. Tony asked, "Was she a dancer too?"	R	B
6. Tess "said, No, not at all."	F	I
7. "I don't" understand, Tony said.	V	N
8. "Did your mother want you to tap-dance?" asked Tony.	T	D
9. "No," said Tess. "She said I would make a great trapper."	H	J
10. Then Tess "said," I guess I heard her wrong!	G	S

Now write each circled letter above on the matching numbered line below.

___ _V_ _G_   _U_   __ __ FOUR __ __ __ __ __
 9   3   6   7   8   2   4   8   2   7   4   3   6   5   10

_F_ __ __ __ __ __
 2   10   9   2   1   10

• A Scouting Skunk •

What does a compass rose show?

Circle the verb that best completes each sentence.
If the verb is in the "Yellow" column, color the matching letter yellow.
If the verb is in the "Blue" column, color the matching letter blue.

	Yellow	Blue
1. Sidney _____ the great outdoors.	enjoys	enjoy
2. Her friends _____ to take her camping.	wants	want
3. They _____ Sidney on a trip.	invite	invites
4. But her parents _____ to let her go.	refuses	refuse
5. Her scout leader _____ it is a bad idea.	says	say
6. Even her dog _____ its head.	shakes	shake
7. Sidney _____ sad.	feel	feels
8. But she and her friends _____.	understand	understands
9. Sidney _____ lost all the time.	get	gets
10. Maybe she _____ to learn how to use a compass!	needs	need

O¹ N² A³
W⁴ T⁵ B⁶ E⁷
X⁸ S⁹ R¹⁰

©The Mailbox® • *Language Arts Practice Galore* • TEC61086 • Key p. 92

48 • Subject-verb agreement •

Pirate Dreams

In what parts of the world has Captain Pete searched for treasure?

Circle the word that best completes each sentence.
Then use the words to solve the puzzle.

1. Captain Pete _____ the seas. sail/sails

2. He and his parrot _____ in charge. is/are

3. Captain Pete _____ the orders. gives/giving

4. His parrot _____ them. repeat/repeats

5. Captain Pete and his crew _____ to find treasures. want/wants

6. They _____ in the sand. dig/digging

7. They also _____ maps. study/studies

8. The pirates _____ to find gold. hope/hopes

9. Captain Pete _____ for jewels. search/searches

10. But all his parrot _____ for is some crackers! wish/wishes

A Banana Split

Draw a line to match each pair of symbols.
Write the resulting compound word below the rule it follows.

view
ny
ness
der
bow

fun
kind
pre
rain
spi

wise
mer
ly
ny
cake

cup
quick
shi
sum
un

Break a compound word between the two words that make it.	Break a word between its prefix and base word.	Break a word between its base word and suffix.	Break a word between the double consonants.	Break a word after a long-vowel sound.
c u p c a k e				

• Buzzing Around •

Color each space.
Use the code.

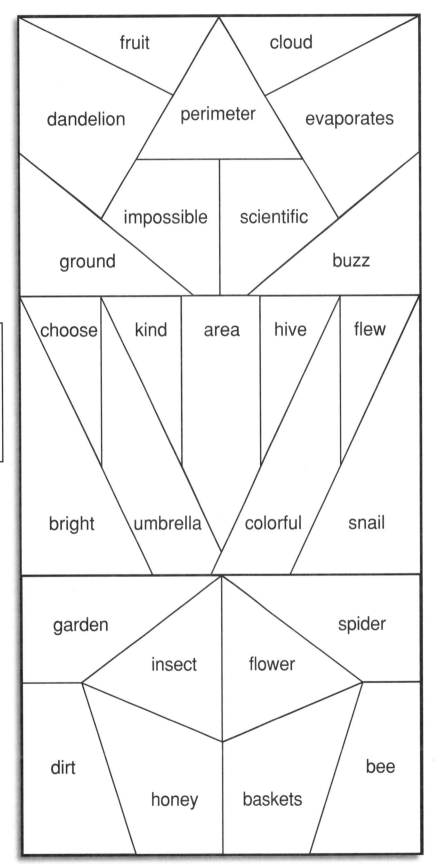

fruit
cloud
dandelion
perimeter
evaporates
impossible
scientific
ground
buzz
choose
kind
area
hive
flew
bright
umbrella
colorful
snail
garden
spider
insect
flower
dirt
bee
honey
baskets

COLOR CODE
one-syllable word = blue
two-syllable word = brown
three-syllable word = green
four-syllable word = red

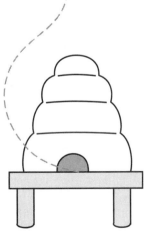

©The Mailbox® • *Language Arts Practice Galore* • TEC61086 • Key p. 92

NAME_____

• Swimming Upstream •

Which waves can fish not swim in?

Look at each row of letters.
Write a letter in the blank to form a compound word.
Circle the compound word.

No Swimming

1.	D	(B	E	C	O	<u>M</u>	E)	R	A	T	M
2.	T	L	U	T	H	___	M	S	E	L	F
3.	A	O	C	U	P	___	A	K	E	C	P
4.	F	W	H	F	I	___	E	F	L	Y	T
5.	C	A	I	R	P	___	R	T	U	R	S
6.	B	I	S	N	O	___	B	A	L	L	G
7.	H	V	N	S	E	___	S	H	O	R	E
8.	I	H	O	W	E	___	E	R	O	W	H
9.	R	Q	C	E	Y	___	L	I	D	T	M
10.	U	L	S	U	N	___	H	I	N	E	J

©The Mailbox® • Language Arts Practice Galore • TEC61086 • Key p. 92

•Keeping Sharp•

Use the code.
Write a word in each shape.
Then make a compound word.

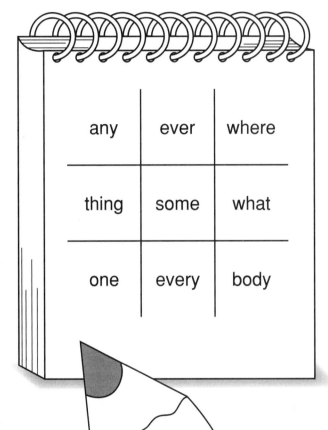

any	ever	where
thing	some	what
one	every	body

1. | any | + | one | = _____

2. ☐ + ☐ = _____

3. ☐ + ☐ = _____

4. ☐ + ☐ = _____

5. ☐ + ☐ = _____

6. ☐ + ☐ = _____

7. ☐ + ☐ = _____

8. ☐ + ☐ = _____

9. ☐ + ☐ = _____

10. ☐ + ☐ = _____

• In the Spotlight •

Why does Hannah Hippo dance with a flashlight?

Read each clue.
Write a matching compound word on the lines.

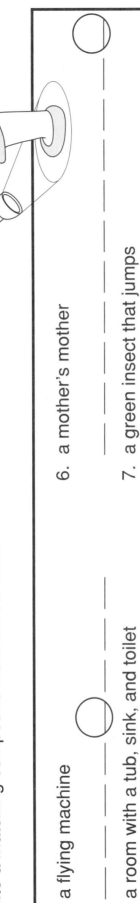

1. a flying machine

   ___ ___ ___ ___ (○) ___ ___ ___ ___ ___

2. a room with a tub, sink, and toilet

   ___ ___ (○) ___ ___ ___ ___ ___ ___

3. what a caterpillar becomes

   ___ ___ ___ ___ (○) ___ ___ ___ ___

4. a handheld tool that gives light

   ___ ___ ___ (○) ___ ___ ___ ___ ___ ___

5. sport with an oval ball

   ___ ___ ___ ___ (○) ___ ___ ___ ___

6. a mother's mother

   ___ ___ ___ ___ ___ (○) ___ ___ ___ ___

7. a green insect that jumps

   ___ ___ ___ (○) ___ ___ ___ ___ ___ ___

8. a movie snack made from corn

   ___ ___ ___ (○) ___ ___ ___ ___

9. a flat, round breakfast food

   ___ ___ ___ (○) ___ ___ ___ ___ ___

10. the day you were born

    ___ ___ ___ ___ ___ ___ (○) ___ ___ ___

Write each circled letter on the matching numbered lines below.

It makes her feel "___ ___ ___ ___ ___ ___ ___ ___ ___ ___"
                      1   10 7   2   3   5   8

___ ___ ___ ___ ___ ___ ___ ___ !
 1   10 4   2   9   6   9   9   3

"Sssweet" Treats

Which snake bakes the best desserts?

Color the boxes that have contractions in them.

c	a	h	p
it's	colors	isn't	shoes
l	i	e	l
they're	covered	smiles	I'm
t	f	o	u
his	it'll	can't	she'll
k	b	h	o
let's	I've	laughed	flies
h	m	n	e
don't	he's	theirs	we're

Write the letters in the remaining boxes in order.

___ " ___ ___ ___ - ___ ___ ___ ___ "

NAME _____

Heading Home

Cut apart the puzzle pieces along the dotted lines.
Sort out the pieces that have correctly spelled contractions.
Glue each piece on the matching grid space.

Puzzle pieces:

do'nt	wee'v	don't
your'e	she's	we've
they'ave	l'am	willn't
youh've	we're	he's
arn't	you've	l'd
hei's	sh'es	you're
l'ld	won't	l'm
wee'r	aren't	they'll

Grid:

we have	they will	you are	I would
I am	are not	do not	he is
she is	will not	you have	we are

©The Mailbox® • Language Arts Practice Galore • TEC61086 • Key p. 93

• Back Together Again •

Cut apart the puzzle pieces below.
Find the two pieces that make each contraction.
Glue the pieces onto each square.

I'm	we're	can't
you've	let's	she'll
it's	shouldn't	they'd

©The Mailbox® • *Language Arts Practice Galore* • TEC61086 • Key p. 93

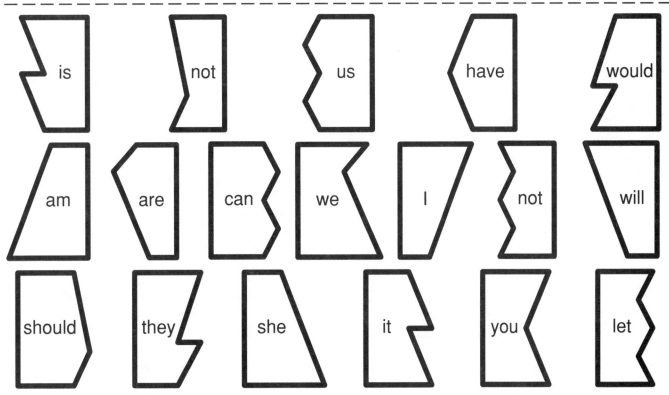

is not us have would

am are can we I not will

should they she it you let

• Contractions • 57

Shine On!

Write *bi*, *mis*, *pre*, or *un* to complete each word.
Color by the code.

Color Code
bi = yellow
mis = black
pre = red
un = blue

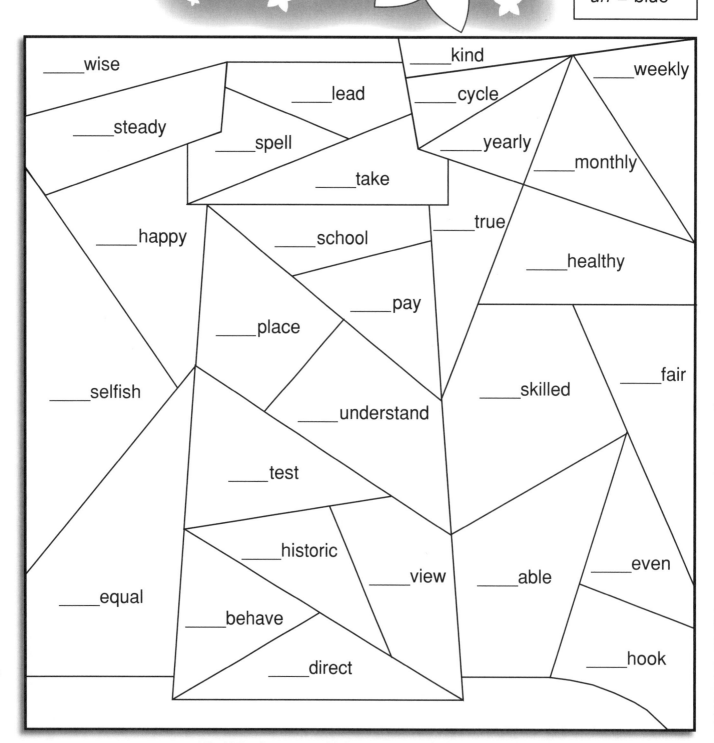

____wise

____kind

____weekly

____lead

____cycle

____steady

____spell

____yearly

____monthly

____take

____happy

____school

____true

____healthy

____pay

____place

____selfish

____skilled

____fair

____understand

____test

____historic

____even

____view

____able

____equal

____behave

____hook

____direct

NAME _____

Aardvark Art

Write *dis-*, *re-*, or *sub-* to make new words.
Circle the new words in the puzzle.

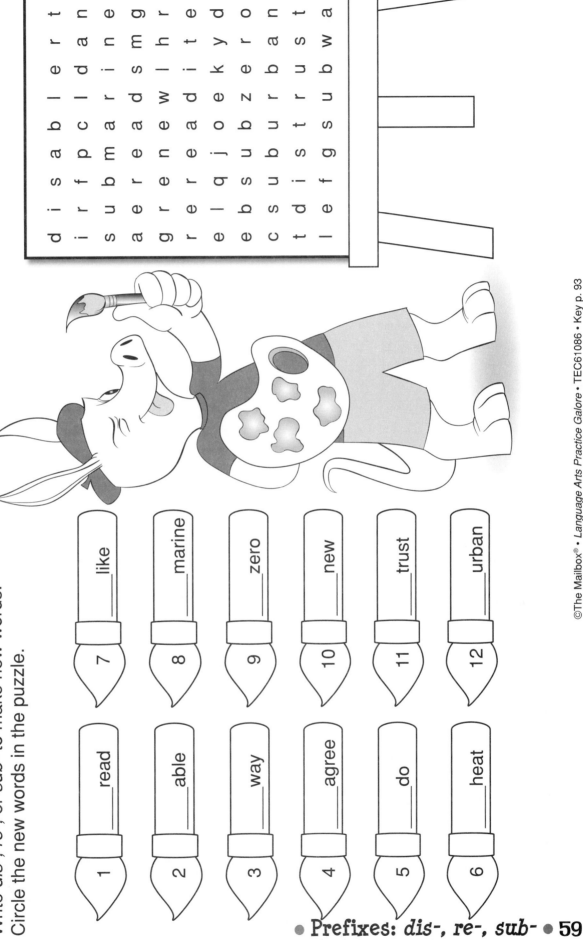

```
d i s a b l e r t y
i r f p c l d a n r
s u b m a r i n e e
a e r e a d s m g h
g r e n e w l h r e
r e l q j o e k y d
e b s u b z e r o d
c s u b u r b a n k
t d i s t r u s t s
l e f g s u b w a y
```

1. ___ read
2. ___ able
3. ___ way
4. ___ agree
5. ___ do
6. ___ heat

7. ___ like
8. ___ marine
9. ___ zero
10. ___ new
11. ___ trust
12. ___ urban

• Open Wide! •

Write a word that begins with *mis-*, *pre-*, *re-*, or *tri-* to match each clue.

1 a shape with three angles

$\underset{14}{\rule{1.5em}{0.4pt}}\ \underset{12}{\rule{1.5em}{0.4pt}}\ \underset{8}{\rule{1.5em}{0.4pt}}\ \underset{1}{a}\ \underset{10}{n}\ \underset{6}{g}\ \underset{9}{l}\ \underset{4}{e}$

2 to write again

___ ___ ___ ___ ___ ___ ___
12 4 17 12 8 14 4

3 to view before

___ ___ ___ ___ ___ ___ ___
11 12 4 16 8 4 17

4 to not trust

___ ___ ___ ___ ___ ___ ___ ___
19 8 13 14 12 15 13 14

5 to finish again

___ ___ ___ ___ ___ ___ ___ ___
12 4 5 8 10 8 13 7

6 to put in a wrong place

___ ___ ___ ___ ___ ___ ___ ___
19 8 13 11 9 1 2 4

7 to cut before

___ ___ ___ ___ ___ ___
11 12 4 2 15 14

8 a cycle with three wheels

___ ___ ___ ___ ___ ___ ___ ___
14 12 8 2 18 2 9 4

How does a dentist clean an alligator's teeth?

To find out, write the matching letters from above on the numbered lines below.

He cleans them

___ ___ ___ ___ , ___ ___ ___ ___
16 4 12 18   16 4 12 18

___ ___ ___ ___ ___ ___ ___ ___ ___ !
2 1 12 4 5 15 9 9 18

• Running on Empty •

How will the car get to the gas pump?

Write *-able* or *-ness* to complete each word.
Then color each word that ends with *-ness* to show the path.

dark____	fix____	shy____	soft____	ill____
good____	slow____	kind____	wash____	sweet____
read____	bend____	break____	pay____	wet____
agree____	drink____	sick____	cold____	hard____
comfort____	remark____	fit____	do____	depend____

• Suffixes: *-able, -ness* • 61

NAME_____

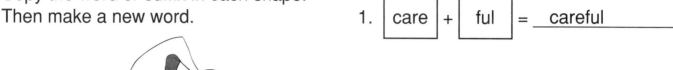

• Cat-in-the-Box •

Use the code.
Copy the word or suffix in each shape.
Then make a new word.

1. | care | + | ful | = ___careful___

2. ⌐ + ⌐ = _____

3. ⌐ + ⌐ = _____

4. ⌐ + ☐ = _____

5. ⌐ + ☐ = _____

6. ⌐ + ⌐ = _____

7. ⌐ + ⌐ = _____

8. ☐ + ☐ = _____

9. ⌐ + ☐ = _____

10. ⌐ + ⌐ = _____

harm	care	less
thank	ful	joy
hope	color	flavor

©The Mailbox® • *Language Arts Practice Galore* • TEC61086 • Key p. 93

• **Suffixes:** *-ful, -less* •

•Peekaboo!•

Write a word that ends with *-ful, -less,* or *-ness* to match each clue.

Across
1. without clouds
3. without weight
7. state of being neat
9. full of taste

Down
1. full of care
2. without spots
3. full of wonder
4. state of being slow
5. state of being still
6. without fear
8. state of being sad
10. full of tears

• Curl Up With a Good Book •

Circle the letter in the column that shows how to make each word plural.
Then write the plural noun.

	add -s	add -es	
1. fox	H	(R)	foxes
2. wish	C	U	
3. car	E	F	
4. dress	K	I	
5. shoe	S	B	
6. watch	A	V	
7. glass	L	N	
8. lunch	E	D	
9. kid	C	I	
10. bus	J	O	
11. game	H	D	
12. box	G	T	

Where do books like to sleep?

Write the circled letters on the matching numbered lines.

___ ___ ___ ___   ___ ___ ___
2   7   8   3   1   12 11 3   4   1

___ ___ ___ ___ ___
9   10 6   3   1   5

A Path for Panda

Which dinner will the panda eat?

Color the box that shows each word's correctly spelled plural form.

BAMBOO KING

1. family	familys	familyes	families
2. penny	pennyes	pennies	pennys
3. story	stories	storys	storris
4. daisy	daisys	daisies	daisyes
5. baby	babis	babys	babies
6. candy	candees	candies	candys
7. lady	ladies	ladis	ladys
8. party	parties	partys	partees
9. cherry	cherrys	cherries	cherryes
10. berry	berrees	berries	berrys

Color the dinner at the bottom of the column that has the most colored boxes.

• Plurals: changing *y* to *i* • 65

• A Piece of Cake •

Unscramble the letters to form each word's plural form.
Then circle the new words in the puzzle.

w	o	l	v	e	s	c	b	g	l	o	q	e	x
a	c	r	x	c	s	a	q	r	t	i	h	r	h
f	p	i	y	h	s	l	o	y	h	p	w	l	w
u	m	z	l	e	a	v	e	s	i	k	i	v	s
k	p	j	i	b	t	e	k	h	e	l	v	e	s
h	a	l	v	e	s	s	n	w	v	b	e	e	g
u	v	e	e	f	n	k	i	a	e	t	s	d	n
n	d	j	s	h	e	l	v	e	s	d	o	a	j
f	a	s	c	a	r	v	e	s	n	c	r	c	m
z	m	l	o	a	v	e	s	v	g	i	d	p	s

1. leaf   easelv

2. wolf   owvsle

3. shelf   lseehvs

4. half   lahsve

5. thief   ieethvs

6. calf   claves

7. knife   kesniv

8. elf   vlese

9. loaf   lasove

10. life   ivlse

NAME_____

Keeping the Beat

Use the code to write each word's plural form.

1. ox

2. goose

3. mouse

4. tooth

5. foot

6. man

7. woman

8. child

9. cactus

10. sheep

a c d e f g h

i l m n o p

r s t w x

• Traffic Jam •

Why is Officer Centipede always asked to help?

Read each sentence.
Circle the best answer.
If the answer is in the "Yellow" column, color the matching numbered section in the puzzle yellow.
If the answer is in the "Blue" column, color the matching numbered section in the puzzle blue.

	Yellow	Blue
1. There is a traffic jam in the _____ center.	town's	towns
2. Three _____ are blowing their horns.	car's	cars
3. A _____ wheels are screeching.	truck's	trucks
4. The _____ are getting hot.	driver's	drivers
5. The police _____ phones begin ringing.	stations	station's
6. Two _____ send their best cops to help.	departments	department's
7. Officer _____ whistle blows.	Crickets	Cricket's
8. Officer _____ signs direct traffic.	Centipedes	Centipede's
9. Soon the _____ are safe again.	streets	street's
10. Everything is clear because the _____ came to help.	officers	officer's

He is very _____.

Grandpa's ties | **Grandpas ties** | **Grandmas' knitting** | **Grandma's knitting**

Uncle Kurts tools | Uncle Kurt's tools | Aunt Karlas hats | Aunt Karla's hats

Mom's books | Moms' books | Dad's golf clubs | Dads golf clubs

Ken's coins | Kens coins | Kathy shoes | Kathy's shoes

Kevins cars | Kevin's cars | my sister's dolls | my sisters dolls

my nieces pets | my niece's pets | Kirbys' blocks | Kirby's blocks

---

All in the Family

How will everyone's stuff fit in Kirby's house?

Cut out the puzzle pieces along the dotted lines.

Sort to find the pieces that are written correctly.

Glue each piece on the matching grid space.

	Grandpa	Grandma
Uncle Kurt	Mom	My brother, Kevin
Cousin Ken	Aunt Karla	Cousin Kathy
	My niece, Kate	Me, Kirby

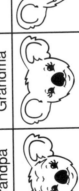
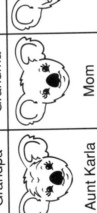

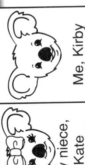

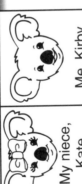

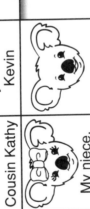
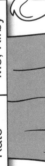

Dad

My sister, Kendra

• Minding His Manners •

What did the teddy bear say when he was offered dessert?

Underline the pronoun that could replace the underlined word or words. Write the matching letter or letters in the puzzle, one letter in each box.

N	O		1		2		3		.
4	,			5	6	7		8		!

1. <u>Barry's</u> friend Beth is coming to dinner.

   (TH)   his   (CL)   their

2. He is cooking <u>Beth's</u> favorite food, baked fish.

   (AP)   his   (AN)   her

3. <u>Barry and Beth's</u> plan is to eat at 6:00.

   (KS)   their   (MY)   our

4. <u>Barry's</u> oven is not working correctly.

   (IM)   His   (AP)   My

5. Barry hopes Beth is not surprised by <u>the fish's</u> color.

   (LM)   our   (ST)   its

6. He wants Beth to like <u>the dinner's</u> taste.

   (U)   its   (Y)   their

7. Luckily for Barry, it was <u>Beth's</u> idea to bring dessert.

   (TT)   his   (FF)   her

8. Maybe <u>Barry and Beth's</u> dinner won't be ruined after all.

   (ED)   their   (ON)   our

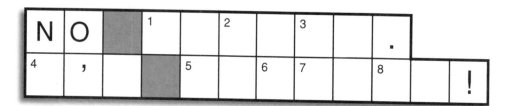

NAME

• A Boa's Bones •

Cut out the puzzle pieces along the dotted lines.
Match each piece to its synonym.
Glue the pieces on the chart.

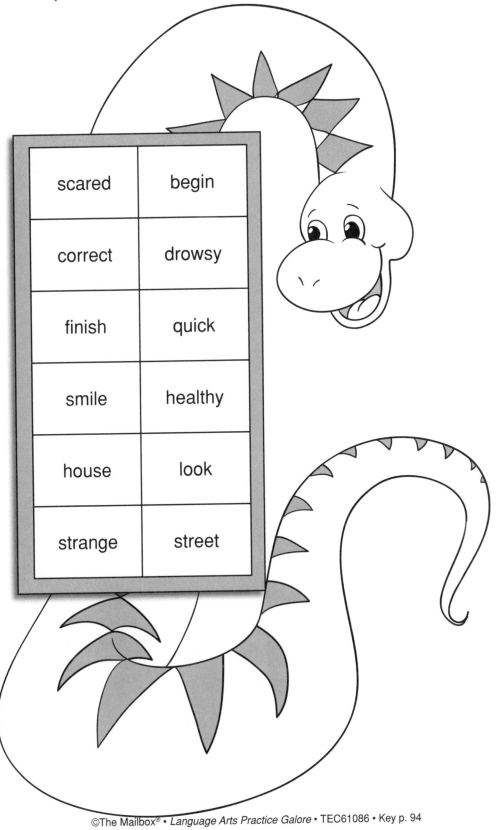

scared	begin
correct	drowsy
finish	quick
smile	healthy
house	look
strange	street

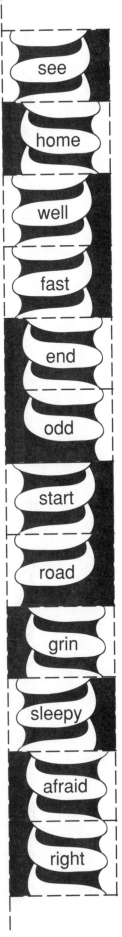

see

home

well

fast

end

odd

start

road

grin

sleepy

afraid

right

To the Moon!

Write a synonym for each word.
Circle the synonym in the puzzle.

1. automobile

2. difficult

3. leap

4. below

5. simple

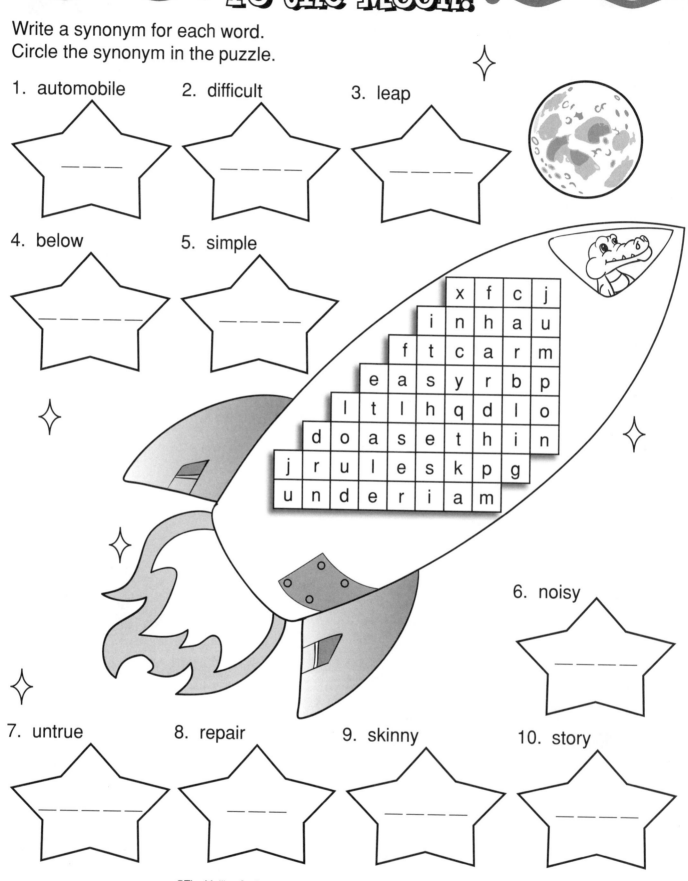

x	f	c	j
i	n	h	a	u
f	t	c	a	r	m
e	a	s	y	r	b	p
l	t	l	h	q	d	l	o
d	o	a	s	e	t	h	i	n
j	r	u	l	e	s	k	p	g
u	n	d	e	r	i	a	m

6. noisy

7. untrue

8. repair

9. skinny

10. story

• Fun and Games •

What is an otter's favorite game to play?

Write a synonym for each word.
Use the word bank to help you.

Word Bank

right	mad
late	talk
alike	run
buy	smart
finish	large

1. same __ __ __ __ ◯__

    2. angry ◯__ __ __

3. big __ ◯__ __ __ __

    4. purchase __ ◯__ __

5. correct __ __ __ ◯__ __

    6. chat ◯__ __ __ __

7. intelligent __ __ ◯__ __

    8. tardy __ __ ◯__ __

9. jog __ __ ◯__

    10. end __ __ ◯__ __ __ __

Write each circled letter on the matching numbered line below.

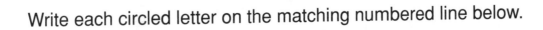

"
___ ___ ___ ___ ___ ___ ___ ___ ___ ___ ___ ___ "!
 9   3   2   1   8   5   7   8   6   4   10   3

Singing for His Supper

Write an antonym for each word.
Then write the words in order from left to right along the chain, one letter in each circle.
Some letters have been filled in for you.

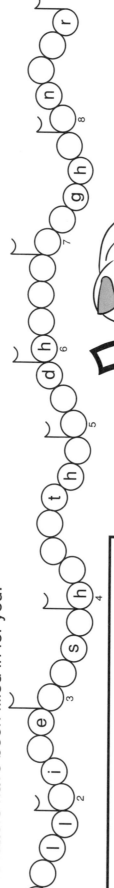

① (l) (i) (e) (s) (h) (t) (h) (d) (h) (g) (h) (n) (r)
1   2   3   4   5   6   7   8

Braxton

1. short ___ ___ ___

2. narrow ___ ___ ___ ___

3. found ___ ___ ___ ___

4. sick ___ ___ ___ ___ ___

5. young ___ ___ ___

6. soft ___ ___ ___ ___

7. left ___ ___ ___ ___ ___

8. over ___ ___ ___ ___ ___

Opposites Attract

Write an antonym for each word.
Solve the puzzle.

Across
1. over
4. wide
7. remember
8. yell
9. lose
10. go

Down
2. old
3. wet
4. quiet
5. save
6. tall
7. smile

• A Big Dig •

What is as big as a dinosaur but weighs nothing?

Circle the antonym for each word.
If the antonym is in the "Yellow" column, color the letter yellow.
If the antonym is in the "Blue" column, color the letter blue.

		Yellow	Blue
1.	frown	smile	growl
2.	give	lend	take
3.	loose	baggy	tight
4.	noisy	loud	quiet
5.	play	work	join
6.	polite	nice	rude
7.	rough	bumpy	smooth
8.	sour	bitter	sweet
9.	tame	broken	wild
10.	whisper	murmur	yell
11.	save	keep	spend
12.	poor	rich	broke

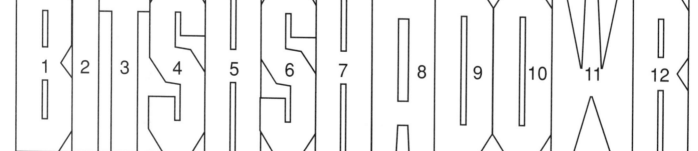

• Anchors Aweigh! •

If the words in each pair are antonyms,
   color the box blue.
If the words in each pair are synonyms,
   color the box red.

above below	destroy build	big small	throw toss	come go	day night	asleep awake
enemy friend	chilly cold	glad happy	stroll walk	dirty unclean	above over	cold hot
backward forward	early late	cry laugh	jog run	bad good	dry wet	begin finish
deep shallow	alike different	close open	fight argue	down up	add subtract	fancy plain
find discover	few many	pretty ugly	shout yell	crooked straight	fat thin	small tiny
fast slow	many several	buy sell	incorrect wrong	false true	wet soggy	found lost
catch miss	frown smile	surprised startled	keep save	tidy neat	float sink	clean dirty

• Synonyms and antonyms • 77

• Two of a Kind •

Find a synonym and an antonym for each word.
Write each word in the matching letter boxes.
Use the word bank to help you.

Synonym		Antonym
1.	wet	
2.	several	
3.	smile	
4.	filthy	
5.	purchase	
6.	right	
7.	over	
8.	find	

WORD BANK

above
buy
clean
correct
dirty
discover
dry
few

frown
grin
lose
many
sell
soggy
under
wrong

Hip Hip Hooray!

What kind of cereal does Chelsea eat each morning?

Circle the word that matches each meaning.
Then fill in the puzzle with the letters by your answers, writing
one letter in each box.

1		2		3		4	5		
" 6		7		8	" 9		10	!	

1. a honey-making insect
   - (TH) be
   - (SH) bee

2. the evening
   - (E) night
   - (O) knight

3. correct
   - (OA) write
   - (EA) right

4. a breakfast food
   - (T) cereal
   - (R) serial

5. they are
   - (S) they're
   - (Y) there

6. 60 minutes
   - (CH) hour
   - (BR) our

7. not strong
   - (OW) week
   - (EE) weak

8. to put on
   - (D) where
   - (R) wear

9. stop so someone can catch up
   - (OU) weight
   - (IO) wait

10. one more than three
   - (N) for
   - (S) four

Picking a Pair

Write a homophone for each word.
Circle the homophone in the puzzle.

1.  eight _ _ _ _

2. knew _ _ _

3. our _ _ _ _

4. would _ _ _ _ _

5. 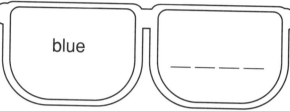 blue _ _ _ _

6.  pair _ _ _ _

7. 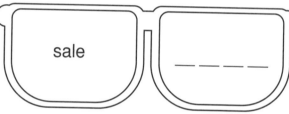 sale _ _ _ _

8. 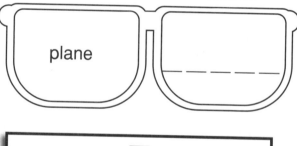 plane _ _ _ _ _

E							
e	t	s	n	h	a	p	x
p	e	a	r	n	v	l	p
b	m	i	g	e	i	a	f
s	b	l	e	w	q	i	o
d	r	j	b	u	z	n	a
y	l	a	w	o	o	d	t
h	o	u	r	c	k	w	e

• Fancy Flying •

Unscramble the letters to make a homophone for each word.
Write the homophone in the letter boxes.

Sail Into the Sale at the Pale Pail.

1. hole   l e w o h

2. nose   n w k s o

3. deer   r e d a

4. through   h r w t e

5. sun   n s o

6. meet   a t m e

7. hear   r e e h

8. plain   n l a p e

9. piece   p c a e e

10. right   r t w e i

11. not   k o t n

12. board   d r o e b

• Smooth Sailing •

Add *ed* to each base word.
Color by the code.

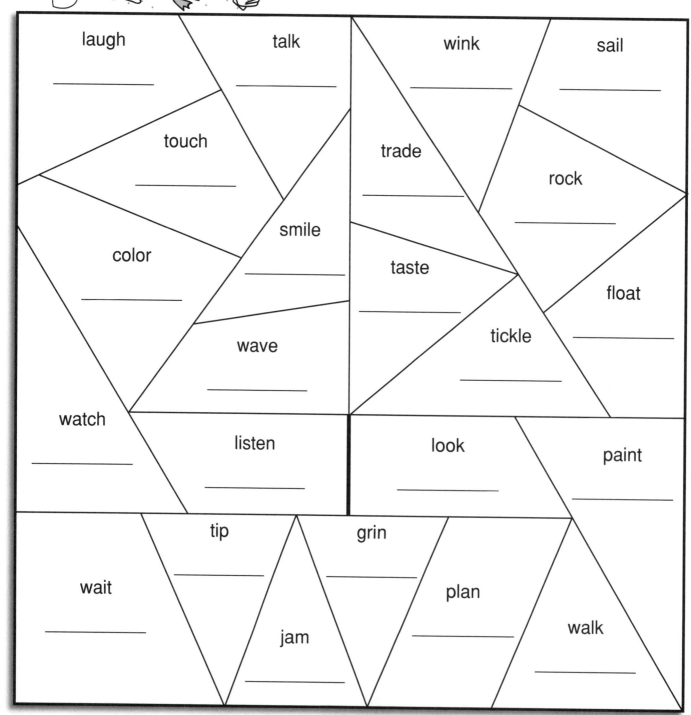

laugh

talk

wink

sail

touch

trade

rock

smile

color

taste

float

wave

tickle

watch

listen

look

paint

tip

grin

wait

plan

jam

walk

• A Tall Order •

How will the cow get to the ice cream truck?

Circle each word that is spelled correctly.
Connect the circled words.

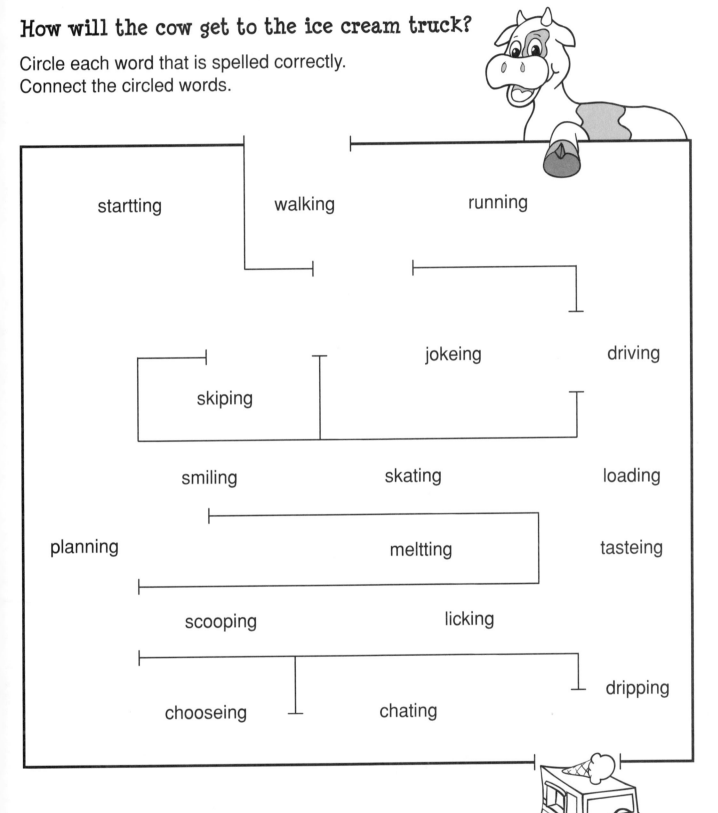

startting   walking   running

                        jokeing   driving

    skiping

smiling   skating   loading

planning   meltting   tasteing

    scooping   licking

                                    dripping

    chooseing   chating

Announcing Anagrams!

Unscramble each word below to make another word.

1. tab   _____
2. loop   _____
3. rats   _____
4. name   _____
5. sore   _____
6. was   _____
7. pam   _____
8. slit   _____

Write each new word next to its definitions.

1. _____ a fiery ball in space; the main performer in a play

2. _____ a tool with teeth; past tense of see

3. _____ a body of water; to come together to do something

4. _____ a series of words on paper; to write a series of words

5. _____ a flower; a pink or red color

6. _____ a small flying mammal; a piece of wood used to hit a ball

7. _____ unkind, wicked; to matter

8. _____ a drawing of an area; making a drawing of an area

NAME_____

• A Busy Shopping Day •

Complete each pair of sentences by writing the same word on each blank.
Circle the word in the puzzle.

1. Where should we _____ the car?

   Let's leave it by the _____ .

2. Look at all of the fall _____ !

   Hurry, we have to get to the store before everyone _____ .

3. We can buy some _____ to put on our toast.

   Let's _____ all we can in our shopping cart.

4. _____ I buy something to drink?

   You can buy a _____ of juice.

5. Please _____ up our groceries now.

   Wait, my _____ finger is stuck in the shopping cart!

Joe's Foods

l	f	i	b	c	m	e
e	n	r	i	n	g	j
a	b	k	t	g	a	c
v	h	d	j	a	m	a
e	p	a	r	k	l	n
s	l	b	f	i	t	o

NAME_____

• Sightseeing •

Complete each pair of sentences by writing
   the same word on each blank.
Write the words in order from left to right
   along the chain, one letter in each circle.

1. I'm glad we could _____ the dog to sit in the car.

   Listen to the _____ whistle!

2. I'd like to _____ the train pass.

   Will you look at your _____ and tell me the time?

3. Look at that big _____!

   I'd like to ride in a boat and _____ on the waves.

4. Can we walk _____ the hill to the shore?

   I'd like to feel the soft _____ on that duck.

5. Can we take another trip in the month of _____?
   Yes, but now let's _____ back to the car.

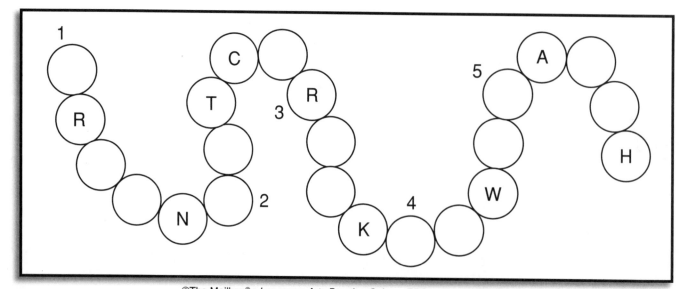

86 • **Multiple-meaning words** •

Answer Keys

Page 4

1. Pablo Penguin is an <u>expert</u> <u>acrobat</u>.
2. First, he warms up by <u>stretching</u> his <u>legs</u>.
3. <u>Second</u>, he <u>flaps</u> his wings.
4. <u>Then</u> he <u>dashes</u> about doing his tricks.
5. He <u>bends</u> and flips, and then <u>stands</u> on his head.
6. Pablo is the South Pole's <u>best-kept</u> secret.
7. Are you <u>planning</u> a trip to <u>Antarctica</u>?
8. Be sure to <u>catch</u> his <u>act</u>!

S	T	A	N	D	S	B	G	D
T	E	D	A	S	H	E	S	A
R	K	E	B	F	K	T	C	N
E	X	P	E	R	T	D	A	T
T	H	E	N	F	B	S	T	A
C	H	F	S	P	J	N	C	R
H	A	L	E	G	S	A	H	C
I	C	A	C	R	O	B	A	T
N	T	P	O	S	M	U	Q	I
G	O	S	N	C	R	T	T	C
B	E	N	D	S	G	M	L	A
I	P	L	A	N	N	I	N	G
B	E	S	T	K	E	P	T	Y

Page 5

b<u>o</u>x Y	l<u>i</u>d R	m<u>o</u>p Y	f<u>i</u>sh R	r<u>i</u>ch R	g<u>i</u>ft R	h<u>o</u>nk Y
bl<u>o</u>ck Y	m<u>i</u>lk R	pl<u>o</u>p Y	fr<u>o</u>g Y	p<u>o</u>nd Y	d<u>i</u>p R	l<u>o</u>ng Y
r<u>o</u>cket Y	w<u>i</u>ng R	fl<u>o</u>ss Y	th<u>i</u>s R	sw<u>i</u>ng R	tr<u>i</u>ck R	m<u>o</u>m Y
m<u>o</u>th Y	br<u>i</u>ng R	up<u>o</u>n Y	h<u>i</u>m R	h<u>o</u>pping Y	d<u>o</u>t Y	s<u>o</u>cks Y
st<u>o</u>p Y	tr<u>i</u>p R	s<u>o</u>ccer Y	h<u>i</u>d R	ch<u>i</u>n R	w<u>i</u>sh R	fr<u>o</u>st Y

Page 6

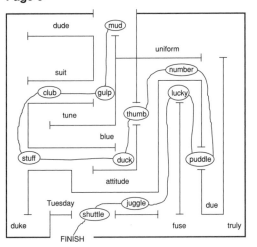

Page 7

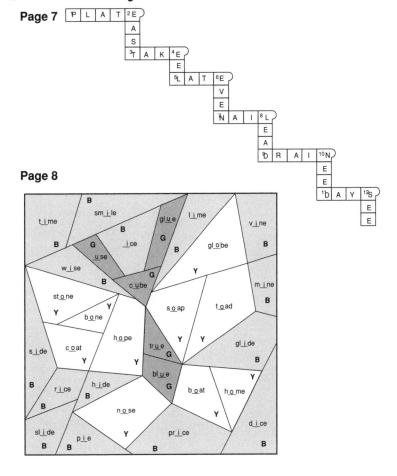

Page 8

t<u>i</u>me, sm<u>i</u>le, gl<u>u</u>e, l<u>i</u>me, v<u>i</u>ne, <u>i</u>ce, gl<u>o</u>be, u<u>s</u>e, c<u>u</u>be, w<u>i</u>se, m<u>i</u>ne, st<u>o</u>ne, b<u>o</u>ne, s<u>o</u>ap, t<u>o</u>ad, h<u>o</u>pe, s<u>i</u>de, c<u>o</u>at, tr<u>u</u>e, gl<u>i</u>de, bl<u>u</u>e, h<u>i</u>de, b<u>o</u>at, h<u>o</u>me, r<u>i</u>ce, n<u>o</u>se, d<u>i</u>ce, sl<u>i</u>de, p<u>i</u>e, pr<u>i</u>ce

Page 9

1. that
2. hat
3. cat
4. mat
5. man
6. fan
7. pan
8. tan
9. tap
10. map
11. nap
12. snap

Page 10

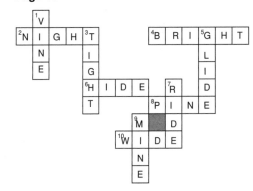

Page 11

1. rest
2. spell
3. vest
4. yellow
5. eating
6. treat
7. smell
8. meat
9. wheat
10. shell
11. pest
12. contest

r	g	t	y	o	s	m	e	l	l
e	t	r	e	h	p	n	i	v	s
s	h	e	l	l	e	u	m	e	l
t	z	a	l	p	l	c	e	s	m
e	r	t	o	q	l	j	a	t	p
w	f	d	w	h	e	a	t	a	e
e	a	t	i	n	g	k	b	y	s
x	c	o	n	t	e	s	t	v	t

Page 12

1. hot
2. slot
3. shop
4. rock
5. spot
6. stop
7. locked
8. drop
9. sock
10. not

IT'S "HOP-PERONI"!

	__ale	__in	__ider	__ace	__arf	__eed	__eep
sc	scale				scarf		
sp		spin	spider	space		speed	
sw							sweep

	__im	__arm	__ort	__eak	__ing	__ark	__alp
sc							scalp
sp			sport	speak		spark	
sw	swim	swarm			swing		

Page 14

1. John is a produce farmer.
2. He loves to ride on his tractor.
3. He tries to be outside by sunrise.
4. Then he travels through his fields.
5. His tractor turns the dark brown soil.
6. John loves the bright sunshine.
7. He also likes the warm breezes.
8. He smiles as he prepares the fields.
9. John takes pride in his work.

Page 15

1. ant
2. and
3. land
4. lend
5. send
6. sent
7. bent
8. went
9. want
10. wand
11. sand
12. stand

Page 16

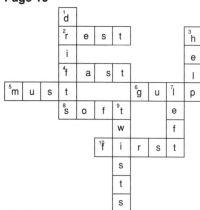

Crossword answers:
1. d
2. rest
3. h
4. fast
5. must
6. gulp
7. l
8. soft
9. t
10. first
(down entries include: dift/drift, heslt... , twfs...)

Page 17

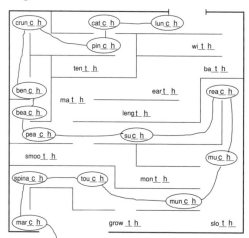

crunch, catch, lunch, pinch, with, tenth, bath, bench, earth, reach, beach, math, length, peach, such, smooth, much, spinach, touch, month, march, munch, growth, sloth

Page 18

Y	G	G	G	G	G
month	trash	push	flush	ash	splash
cloth	fish	teeth	fifth	truth	wreath
fourth	both	mouth	brush	flash	tenth
bush	cash	slush	dish	wash	sixth
earth	ninth	blush	dash	lash	tooth
rash	north	path	health	booth	south

Page 19

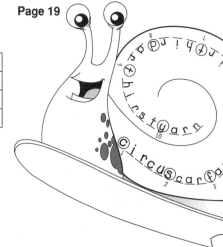

circuscarffarmarchairthirstyarn

Page 20

1. Farmer Brown was worried about his pony, Popcorn.
2. Last Thursday, he noticed something odd.
3. The pony's mane and tail were purple!
4. There was another change the next morning.
5. Popcorn's coat had turned from brown to white.
6. Well, he knew that wasn't normal!
7. Farmer Brown hurried to call the vet.
8. By the time the vet arrived, there was one more change.
9. What a surprise!
10. Popcorn had grown a horn.
11. "I don't know what you were feeding your horse," said the vet.
12. "But now you've got a unicorn!"

U	H	P	O	P	C	O	R	N	T	E	T	W
N	U	K	T	U	B	A	F	O	U	D	H	O
I	R	M	O	R	E	O	U	R	R	F	U	R
C	R	H	G	P	Z	R	Q	M	N	O	R	R
O	I	O	O	L	H	S	V	A	E	A	S	I
R	E	R	C	E	P	E	N	L	D	E	D	E
N	D	N	S	U	R	P	R	I	S	E	A	D
M	O	R	N	I	N	G	C	U	H	J	Y	B

Page 21

1. underwater
2. wonder
3. mermaid
4. summer
5. discover
6. undercover

Page 22

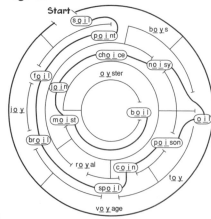

Start → soil, point, boys, choice, noisy, foil, oyster, join, boil, oil, joy, moist, poison, broil, royal, coin, toy, spoil, voyage

Page 23

1. about
2. house
3. town
4. round
5. found
6. frown
7. power
8. south
9. shower
10. growl
11. proud
12. allow

Page 24

	Subject	Predicate	Neither
1. Matilda is a monkey.	K	(S)	D
2. She lives in the jungle.	(I)	L	R
3. Matilda likes swinging in the trees.	N	E	(D)
4. Yellow bananas are her favorite food.	(O)	A	G
5. Many monkeys swing and eat bananas.	B	S	(W)
6. But Matilda is special.	M	(T)	F
7. She knows how to yo-yo!	H	(N)	O
8. Matilda can hold a yo-yo in each hand.	(U)	T	E
9. Her tail can hold a third yo-yo!	R	C	(P)
10. Matilda's tricks are amazing!	(A)	J	Q

IT has ITS UPS AND DOWNS!

Page 25

1. The neighborhood \C/ birds \A/ are all aflutter.

2. A new \K/ surprise \P/ is here.

3. Mrs. Briar \T/ put a birdbath \D/ in her garden.

4. It \B/ is \U/ beautiful!

5. The birds \L/ are \R/ all lining up.

6. The chickadees \O/ have brought \B/ their own towels.

7. A cardinal \M/ brought \R/ some bubble bath.

8. Feathers \T/ are flying with \E/ excitement.

9. Tweeting \I/ can be \B/ heard all over.

10. The birds \R/ hope Mrs. Briar will remember to put \U/ water in the birdbath.

A RUBBER DUCK

Page 26

1. Dr. Tim Chase and Mr. (bill, Bill) Fast are racecar drivers.
   Ⓐ Ⓑ

2. (Dr., dr.) Chase's car is bright blue.
   Ⓐ Ⓑ

3. Mr. (Fast, fast) drives a red car.
   Ⓐ Ⓑ

4. Dr. Chase's son, (mark, Mark), helps his dad.
   Ⓐ Ⓑ

5. The racetrack mechanic is (Mrs., mrs.) Swift.
   Ⓐ Ⓑ

6. Mrs. Swift helps (Bill, bill) and Tim keep their cars running.
   Ⓐ Ⓑ

7. The man who pumps the gasoline is (mr., Mr.) Quick.
   Ⓐ Ⓑ

8. Mr. Quick has a helper named (Tammy, tammy).
   Ⓐ Ⓑ

9. Mr. (quick, Quick) and Tammy work hard at the track.
   Ⓐ Ⓑ

10. Dr. Chase and (mr., Mr.) Fast have lots of help, and they're ready to race!
    Ⓐ Ⓑ

Color the racecar that finished first!

Page 27

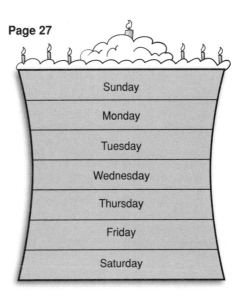

Sunday

Monday

Tuesday

Wednesday

Thursday

Friday

Saturday

Page 28

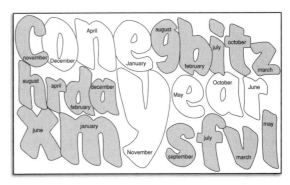

Page 29

Fourth of July	Hanukkah	Thanksgiving	St. Patrick's Day	Valentine's Day
	CELEBRATE!			
Columbus Day	Easter	Halloween	New Year's Eve	Kwanzaa

Page 30

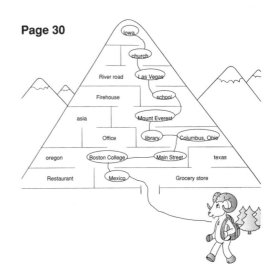

Page 31

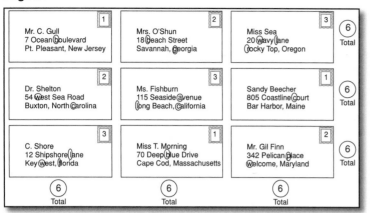

Mr. C. Gull **1** 7 Ocean(b)oulevard Pt. Pleasant, New Jersey	Mrs. O'Shun **2** 18(b)each Street Savannah, (g)eorgia	Miss Sea **3** 20(w)avy(l)ane (r)ocky Top, Oregon
Dr. Shelton **2** 54(w)est Sea Road Buxton, North(c)arolina	Ms. Fishburn **3** 115 Seaside(a)venue (l)ong Beach,(c)alifornia	Sandy Beecher **1** 805 Coastline(c)ourt Bar Harbor, Maine
C. Shore **3** 12 Shipshore(l)ane Key(w)est,(f)lorida	Miss T. Morning **1** 70 Deep(b)lue Drive Cape Cod, Massachusetts	Mr. Gil Finn **2** 342 Pelican(p)lace (w)elcome, Maryland

6 Total (for each column and each row)

Page 32

1. !
2. ?
3. .
4. .
5. ?
6. .
7. !
8. ?
9. !

In a
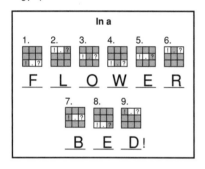

F L O W E R

B E D!

Page 33

	!	.	?
1. Boy, Harry loves to travel	!		
2. He has been all over Africa and Asia	!		
3. Have you ever been to a different country			?
4. You need to get a passport before you go		.	
5. Your passport is stamped in each country you visit		.	
6. Wow, Harry's passport has 43 stamps	!		
7. He'll need a new one soon		.	
8. Do you travel like Harry does			?
9. Harry travels by plane, train, and boat		.	
10. All of this traveling makes him tired		.	
11. Can you guess where Harry will go next			?
12. I think he'll go to sleep		.	

Page 34

Charlie just opened a restaurant.	statement
Have you seen the menu?	question
There are so many choices!	exclamation
Try today's special.	command

Would you rather eat at home?	question
Call Charlie and place an order.	command
Charlie delivers all of the food himself.	statement
Wow, that is *fast* food!	exclamation

Page 35

1. question
2. statement
3. exclamation
4. exclamation
5. command
6. question
7. statement
8. question
9. command

Page 36

under	rabbit	book	farmer
garden	teacher	furry	dirt
quickly	many	joking	hop	school
animal	baby	home	ruler	child
car	lightly	handy	hot	eat
mother	wow	church	mailman	vegetable
pencil	folder	uncle	deeply	beach
grow	to	slowly	the	hat
crunchy	baker	carrot	playground	clown
small	seeds	is	in	sit

Page 37

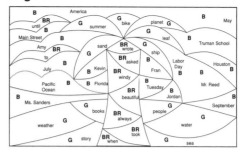

Page 38

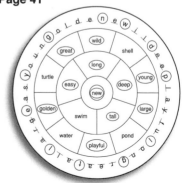

Page 39

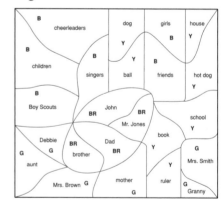

Page 40

Page 41

Page 42

easy	waves	lonely	float	deep	tricky	four
several	bubbled	blue	freeze	little	hid	quiet
windy	keep	pleasant	do	some	salty	hot
cool	took	clever	him	pretty	sat	flipper
green	many	wet	sink	funny	breathe	see

Page 43

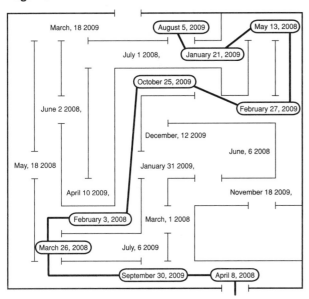

March, 18 2009
August 5, 2009
May 13, 2008
July 1 2008,
January 21, 2009
October 25, 2009
June 2 2008,
February 27, 2009
December, 12 2009
June, 6 2008
May, 18 2008
January 31 2009,
November 18 2009,
April 10 2009,
February 3, 2008
March, 1 2008
March 26, 2008
July, 6 2009
September 30, 2009
April 8, 2008

Page 44

Bryce Canyon, Utah
Durango, Colorado
Santa Fe, New Mexico
Great Falls, Montana
Sedona, Arizona
Cottonwood, California
Valley of Fire, Nevada
Salt Flat, Texas

Can an ant eat a ton of salt?

Page 45

		Yes	No
1.	Bob likes to spend his day resting, eating, and talking.	(U)	V
2.	He likes, to rest in the barn, the field, and the farmhouse.	W	(Z)
3.	He always has a blanket, pillow, and teddy bear with him.	(A)	G
4.	*Warm, relaxed,* and *cozy* are his favorite words!	(L)	P
5.	Bob likes to eat, grain, hay, and grass after a rest.	J	(R)
6.	The, chickens, dogs and horses don't know how he can be so hungry.	K	(B)
7.	They cluck, bark, and nay at him.	(O)	N
8.	Bob just smiles, laughs, and talks, back to the animals.	T	(L)
9.	He thinks life on the farm is fun, quiet, and relaxing.	(E)	H
10.	You would too if you spent each day, resting eating, and talking!	F	(D)

A "BULLDOZER"

Page 46

1. "Are you going to the circus? E asked Shelly. P
2. F I would not D miss it," said Sandy.
3. "The octopus is a great juggler! C Shelly G said.
4. Sandy said, S Yes, U he is amazing to see."
5. R Shelly asked, "Which act is your favorite? N
6. "That is hard to say, T Sandy said. J
7. L I like when the shrimp ride B the sea horses," Shelly said.
8. "I like the lionfish tamer! H Sandy said. A
9. W Well, K what are we waiting for?" Shelly asked.
10. Sandy smiled W and said, T Let's go!"

THE CLOWNFISH

Page 47

		Yes	No
1.	"How did you become a great dancer, Tess?" asked Tony.	(E)	C
2.	Tess said, "Practice, practice, practice."	(O)	L
3.	"But what made you choose tap?" Tony asked.	(A)	M
4.	My mom helped me choose it "said Tess."	K	(P)
5.	Tony asked, "Was she a dancer too?"	(R)	B
6.	Tess "said, No, not at all."	F	(I)
7.	I don't understand, Tony said.	V	(N)
8.	"Did your mother want you to tap-dance?" asked Tony.	(T)	D
9.	"No," said Tess. "She said I would make a great trapper."	(H)	J
10.	Then Tess "said," I guess I heard her wrong!	G	(S)

HAVING TO PUT ON FOUR PAIRS OF SHOES

Page 48

1. enjoys
2. want
3. invite
4. refuse
5. says
6. shakes
7. feels
8. understand
9. gets
10. needs

Page 49

1. sails
2. are
3. gives
4. repeats
5. want
6. dig
7. study
8. hope
9. searches
10. wishes

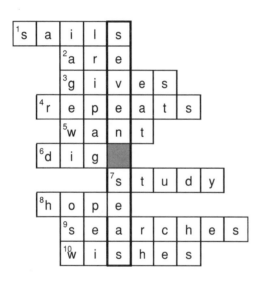

Page 50

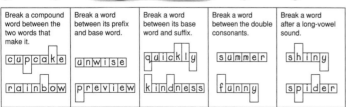

Break a compound word between the two words that make it.	Break a word between its prefix and base word.	Break a word between its base word and suffix.	Break a word between the double consonants.	Break a word after a long-vowel sound.
cup cake	un wise	quick ly	sum mer	shin y
rain bow	pre view	kind ness	fun ny	spi der

Page 51

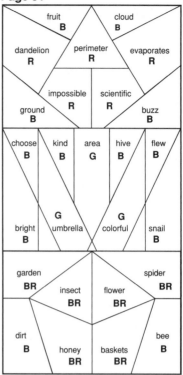

Page 52

1. D (B E C O M E) R A T M
2. T L U T (H I M S E L F)
3. A O (C U P C A K E) C P
4. F W H (F I R E F L Y) T
5. C (A I R P O R T) U R S
6. B I (S N O W B A L L) G
7. H V N (S E A S H O R E)
8. I (H O W E V E R) O W H
9. R Q C (E Y E L I D) T M
10. U L (S U N S H I N E) J

Page 53

1. any + one = anyone
2. some + where = somewhere
3. what + ever = whatever
4. some + thing = something
5. every + body = everybody
6. every + thing = everything
7. some + body = somebody
8. any + thing = anything
9. every + where = everywhere
10. every + one = everyone

Page 54

1. airplane
2. bathroom
3. butterfly
4. flashlight
5. football
6. grandmother
7. grasshopper
8. popcorn
9. pancake
10. birthday

It makes her feel "light" on her feet!

Page 55

c	a	h	p
it's	colors	isn't	shoes
l	i	e	l
they're	covered	smiles	I'm
t	f	o	u
his	it'll	can't	she'll
k	b	h	o
let's	I've	laughed	flies
h	m	n	e
don't	he's	theirs	we're

a "pie-thon"

Page 56

we've	they'll	you're	I'd
I'm	aren't	don't	he's
she's	won't	you've	we're

Page 57

I / am	we / are	can / not
you / have	let / us	she / will
it / is	should / not	they / would

Page 58

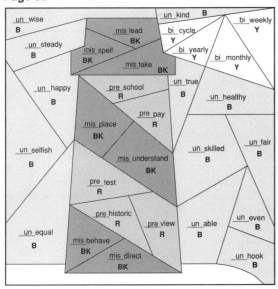

un _ wise **B**
un _ steady **B**
un _ happy **B**
un _ selfish **B**
un _ equal **B**
mis _ lead **BK**
mis _ spell **BK**
mis _ take **BK**
mis _ place **BK**
mis _ understand **BK**
mis _ behave **BK**
mis _ direct **BK**
un _ kind **B**
bi _ cycle **Y**
bi _ yearly **Y**
bi _ monthly **Y**
bi _ weekly **Y**
un _ true **B**
pre _ school **R**
pre _ pay **R**
pre _ test **R**
pre _ historic **R**
pre _ view **R**
un _ healthy **B**
un _ skilled **B**
un _ fair **B**
un _ able **B**
un _ even **B**
un _ hook **B**

Page 59

1. reread
2. disable
3. subway
4. disagree
5. redo
6. reheat
7. dislike
8. submarine
9. subzero
10. renew
11. distrust
12. suburban

```
d i s a b l e r t y
i r f p c l d a n r
s u b m a r i n e e
a e r e a d s m g h
g r e n e w l h r e
r e r e a d i t e a
e l q j o e k y d t
e b s u b z e r o d
c s u b u r b a n k
t d i s t r u s t s
l e f g s u b w a y
```

Page 60

1. triangle
2. rewrite
3. preview
4. mistrust
5. refinish
6. misplace
7. precut
8. tricycle

He cleans them very, very carefully!

Page 61

darkness	fixable	shyness	softness	illness
goodness	slowness	kindness	washable	sweetness
readable	bend able	breakable	pay able	wetness
agreeable	drinkable	sickness	coldness	hardness
comfortable	remarkable	fitness	doable	dependable

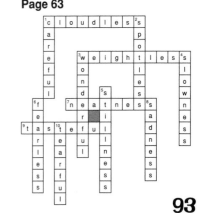

Page 62

1. careful
2. flavorless
3. colorless
4. flavorful
5. joyful
6. hopeless
7. harmless
8. colorful
9. thankful
10. careless

Page 63

```
c l o u d l e s s
a         p
r     w e i g h t l e s s
e     o     l       l
f     n     e       o
u     d   s s       w
l   f n e a t n e s s n
  e   r   i     a   e
t a s t e f u l d n s
r e   u   l     n e s s
i a   l   l     e
l r   f         s
e f   u         s
s u   l
  l
```

Page 64

add -s	add -es	
H	(R)	foxes
C	(U)	wishes
(E)	F	cars
K	(I)	dresses
(S)	B	shoes
A	(V)	watches
L	(N)	glasses
E	(D)	lunches
(C)	I	kids
J	(O)	buses
(H)	D	game
G	(T)	boxes

UNDER THEIR COVERS

Page 65

familys	familyes	families
pennyes	pennies	pennys
stories	storys	storris
daisys	daisies	daisyes
babis	babys	babies
candees	candies	candys
ladies	ladis	ladys
parties	partys	partees
cherrys	cherries	cherryes
berrees	berries	berrys

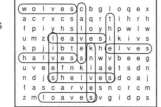

Page 66

1. leaves
2. wolves
3. shelves
4. halves
5. thieves
6. calves
7. knives
8. elves
9. loaves
10. lives

```
w o l v e s c b g l o q e x
a c r x c s a q r t i h r h
f p i y h s l o y h p w l w
u m z l e a v e s i k i v s
k p j i b t e k h e l v e s
h a l v e s n w v b e e g
u v e f n k i a e t s d n
n d j s h e l v e s d o a j
f a s c a r v e s n c r c m
z m l o a v e s v g i d p s
```

Page 67

1. oxen
2. geese
3. mice
4. teeth
5. feet
6. men
7. women
8. children
9. cacti
10. sheep

Page 68

1. town's
2. cars
3. truck's
4. drivers
5. station's
6. departments
7. Cricket's
8. Centipede's
9. streets
10. officers

He is very

Page 69

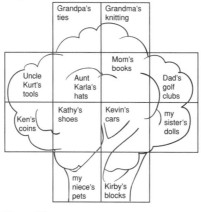

Page 70

N	O		T	H	A	N	K	S	.
I	'	M		S	T	U	F	F	E	D	!

1. Barry's friend Beth is coming to dinner.
   (TH) his   (CL) their

2. He is cooking Beth's favorite food, baked fish.
   (AP) his   (AN) her

3. Barry and Beth's plan is to eat at 6:00.
   (KS) their   (MY) our

4. Barry's oven is not working correctly.
   (IM) His   (AP) My

5. Barry hopes Beth is not surprised by the fish's color.
   (LM) our   (ST) its

6. He wants Beth to like the dinner's taste.
   (U) its   (Y) their

7. Luckily for Barry, it was Beth's idea to bring dessert.
   (TT) his   (FF) her

8. Maybe Barry and Beth's dinner won't be ruined after all.
   (ED) their   (ON) our

Page 71

afraid | start
right | sleepy
end | fast
grin | well
home | see
odd | road

Page 72

1. car
2. hard
3. jump
4. under
5. easy
6. loud
7. false
8. fix
9. thin
10. tale

Page 73

1. alike
2. mad
3. large
4. buy
5. right
6. talk
7. smart
8. late
9. run
10. finish

NAME THAT "TUNA"!

Page 74

1. tall
2. wide
3. lost
4. healthy
5. old
6. hard
7. right
8. under

Page 75

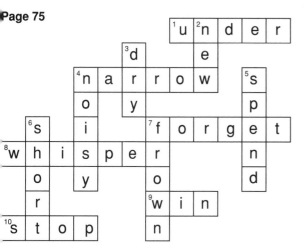

1 Across: under
3 Down: destroy
4 Across: narrow
5 Down: spend
6 Down: sorrow
7 Across: forget
8 Across: whisper
9 Across: win
10 Across: stop

Page 76

1. smile
2. take
3. tight
4. quiet
5. work
6. rude
7. smooth
8. sweet
9. wild
10. yell
11. spend
12. rich

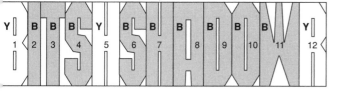

Y	B	B	B	Y	B	S	B	B	B	B	Y
1	2	3	4	5	6	7	8	9	10	11	12

Page 77

B above / below	B destroy / build	B big / small	R throw / toss	B come / go	B day / night	B asleep / awake
B enemy / friend	R chilly / cold	R glad / happy	R stroll / walk	R dirty / unclean	R above / over	B cold / hot
B backward / forward	B early / late	B cry / laugh	R jog / run	B bad / good	B dry / wet	B begin / finish
B deep / shallow	B alike / different	B close / open	R fight / argue	B down / up	B add / subtract	B fancy / plain
R find / discover	B few / many	B pretty / ugly	R shout / yell	B crooked / straight	B fat / thin	R small / tiny
B fast / slow	R many / several	B buy / sell	R incorrect / wrong	B false / true	R wet / soggy	B found / lost
B catch / miss	B frown / smile	R surprised / startled	R keep / save	R tidy / neat	B float / sink	B clean / dirty

Page 78

1. soggy — dry
2. many — few
3. grin — frown
4. dirty — clean
5. buy — sell
6. correct — wrong
7. above — under
8. discover — lose

Page 79

SHE EATS "CHEER" IOS!

1. a honey-making insect
   - TH be
   - SH (bee)
6. 60 minutes
   - CH (hour)
   - BR our

2. the evening
   - E (night)
   - O knight
7. not strong
   - OW week
   - EE (weak)

3. correct
   - OA write
   - EA (right)
8. to put on
   - D where
   - R (wear)

4. a breakfast food
   - T (cereal)
   - R serial
9. stop so someone can catch up
   - OU weight
   - IO (wait)

5. they are
   - S (they're)
   - Y there
10. one more than three
   - N for
   - S (four)

Page 80

1. ate
2. new
3. hour
4. wood
5. blew
6. pear
7. sail
8. plain

		E					
e	t	s	n	h	a	p	x
p	e	a	r	n	v	l	p
b	m	i	g	e	i	a	f
s	b	l	e	w	q	i	o
d	r	j	b	u	z	n	a
y	l	a	w	o	o	d	t
h	o	u	r	c	k	w	e

Page 81
1. whole
2. knows
3. dear
4. threw
5. son
6. meat
7. here
8. plane
9. peace
10. write
11. knot
12. bored

Page 84

1. bat
2. pool
3. star
4. mean
5. rose
6. saw
7. map
8. list

1. star
2. saw
3. pool
4. list
5. rose
6. bat
7. mean
8. map

Page 82

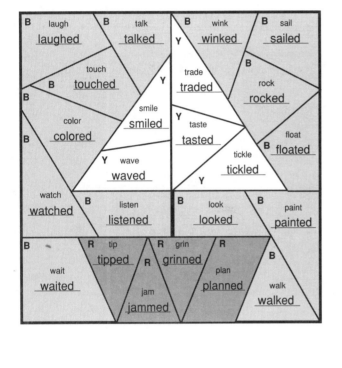

Page 85
1. park
   park

2. leaves
   leaves

3. jam
   jam

4. can
   can

5. ring
   ring

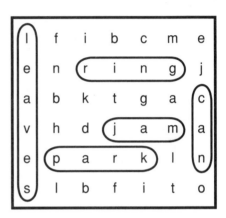

Page 83

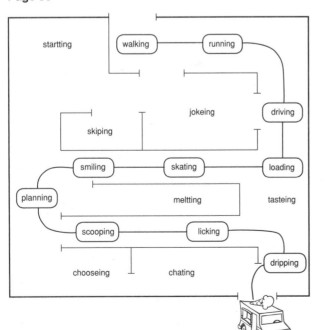

Page 86
1. train
   train

2. watch
   watch

3. rock
   rock

4. down
   down

5. March
   march

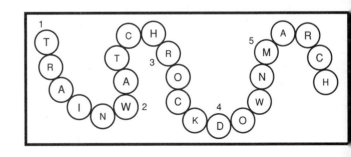